Sam

The
Passing-Out
Parade

Broomsgrove

A Play

Anne Valery

Samuel French — London
www.samuelfrench-london.co.uk

THE PASSING-OUT PARADE

First presented at the Greenwich Theatre in 1979 with the following cast of characters:

Private Diana Smith-Jenkins	Jane Booker
Private Anne Howard	Wendy Morgan
Private Sally Stokes	Janine Duvitski
Private Maureen Crab	Henrietta Baynes
Private Val Davis	Hazel Clyne
Private "Basher" Beasley	Susan Colverd
Private Lil	Polly Hemingway
Sergeant Joyce Pickering	Pat Keen
Corporal Betty Segraves ⎫	
Corporal Broomsgrove ⎬	Charmian May
The C.O. ⎮	
A N.A.A.F.I. Girl ⎭	

and the voices of Tony Church and Anne Valery

The play directed by Jack Emery
Designed by Peter Rice

The action takes place in Pontefract, Yorkshire, in an A.T.S. Barrack Room and in adjoining places

Time: early 1944

AUTHOR'S NOTES

There are very few books about the A.T.S., or indeed any of the Women's Services. Even at the time they were seldom mentioned and on radio were often the butt for jokes. Now—thirty-six years later—it is as if the vast army of girls had never existed, except as a postscript on history. Even the excellent *Picture Post* had only one article about what they actually did. Indeed, one might say that the forgotten army of the last war was not the one in Burma, but the one in skirts.

For the atmosphere of the time, and what women looked like, I suggest *Picture Post 1938–50*, edited by Tom Hopkinson, and *How We Lived Then* by Norman Longmate.

Songs. All the songs mentioned are obtainable on record (see note regarding copyright restrictions for records). However, the songs for the play should be recorded by the cast on a tape-recorder and it is better if they do not sound too professional.

The set. Beds should be truckle or school beds (i.e. iron framed). Preferably, each bed should have a locker which can be bedside tables with a cupboard painted dark brown. Alternatively, shelves painted dark brown with dark green curtains, and shared by two recruits. The walls of the barrack should be a dirty cream, with one or two bricks indicated, and the windows should have criss-cross strips of brown paper, approximately one-and-a-half inches wide, across the panes. Set dressing could include a fire-extinguisher, or better still a stirrup-pump, with a red bucket full of sand. Posters of the A.T.S. or general war-time posters, obtainable from the Imperial War Museum, London, can be used. Family photographs were allowed on the lockers. There should also be a notice on the back of the door. Whatever furniture is used, the Barrack Room must look bleak and shabby.

Uniforms. Skirts should be *slightly* flared and of thick material. Shirts can be men's shirts dyed. The Dylon Advisory Service can help with the correct dyes for khaki. Bloomers should be "old lady" knickers with full leg. Ties—plain cotton khaki; shoes—brown lace-ups. Hats and jackets will probably have to be hired. However, minimum requirements are shirt, tie, skirt and hat. It could be assumed that the rest of the uniform is kept in cupboards outside the room. The marching could take place in a drill hall; all that is needed is the insertion of one line, that due to heavy rain "square bashing" will take place inside.   A.V.

Production Note: In the Greenwich production, the Barrack Room was kept as a standing set and all other scenes were played at the front of the stage, with the Barrack Room in darkness, with relevant pieces of furniture being brought on by members of the cast. The songs of the Chorus were heard played over front-of-house speakers, as was the Epilogue.

DEDICATION

To Paula Milne and Ron C. .lock who commissioned my first play, and gave me the security and encouragement every writer needs. Thank you both.

A.V.

INCIDENTAL MUSIC (Records)

ACT I

"So This Is The Meaning of Heaven"
"Strolling, Just Strolling" (**Flanagan** and **Allen**)
"It's a Lovely Day Tomorrow"
"As Time Goes By"
"Sally" (**Gracie Fields**)

ACT II

"On a Saturday Night" (**Inkspots**)
"You'll Never Know" (**Vera Lynn**)
"Land of Hope and Glory"
"Lily of Laguna"
"Last Post"

ACT I

Scene 1

Chorus Passengers will please refrain from passing water while the train
Is standing in the station—I love you.
But if you really have to function—do not go 'ere Clapham
Junction.
Save it up for bloody towns like Crewe!

Porter (*off, in a Yorkshire accent*) Pontefract. Pontefract Station. Mind the
doors, *if* you please.

*The Recruits enter in the following order: Crab, Beasley, Stokes, David,
Jenkins*

*Private Maureen Crab is twenty-two. She identifies with Rita Hayworth, and
was the leader of a gang at school. The younger girls had "pashes" on her.
She aspires to the lower middle-class. Proudly aware of her physical assets,
she is not as independently minded as she might think: tough and very
sentimental. She wears a wide-shouldered suit, wedge shoes, lace gauntlet
gloves, a frilly blouse and cheap jewellery. She has orange-painted legs and
her hair is a "Rita Hayworth". She carries a tartan gas-mask case and a
bright umbrella. Disgusted, she looks out front*

*Private Basher Beasley is in her late twenties to middle thirties. She is a
gregarious, good-time girl, perhaps as an escape from poverty. Because she is
not attractive, she hides her feelings beneath a brash exterior. She is more
sensitive than one might think. She is chewing gum as she enters. Her clothes
are cheap and cheerful, and her hair is in a turban pinned with a U.S.
Captain's insignia. She carries a battered cardboard gas-mask case*

*Private Sally Stokes is aged between seventeen and nineteen. She has the
pinched look of the chronically undernourished. Her defeated attitude to life
is partly because she has never allowed herself to feel the deep injuries that
have been done to her—it is against her upbringing and her religion. She is
upset by irreverent references to "God" and "Christ", crossing herself when
the Girls use these expressions. Mention of sex upsets her, too. She is the
"obeyer" who might one day ask to be obeyed. She wears old Wellingtons, a
beret and a shabby, navy-blue raincoat which is too small for her. Her gas-
mask is tied with string. She carries a paper carrier-bag*

*Private Val Davis is aged between eighteen and twenty-three. Born and bred
in the East End of London, she will spend the rest of her life there. She enjoys
being the member of a team—before, she was an outsider. She is shabby
though cheerful. Her legs are bare*

*Private Diana Smith-Jenkins is nineteen, and upper middle-class. She is self-
sufficient to the point of appearing arrogant. Nothing will change her. She is*

immaculately groomed and never without a nail file and clean handkerchief. She wears a tweed suit, cream blouse, suede gloves, a felt hat and brogue shoes

As Stokes enters the bottom of her carrier-bag splits, spilling out sandwiches, combinations, a Bible, rosary and cross. Beasley looks back

Beasley Hey! You've dumped your dinner.

Stokes gathers her things up, ashamed

> *Davis bumps into her as she enters*

Davis Sorry. Here, won't take a tick.
Stokes (*muttering*) I can manage. Thanks.

> *Jenkins saunters on, staring straight ahead, then glances back as if looking for someone*

The other girls look around, wondering where to go

> *Sergeant Joyce Pickering appears and steps forward. She is in her forties. Born in Worcestershire, she joined the A.T.S. on the first day of the war, copying her father, who did so in 1914. She cares passionately for classical music. She collects boxes though she has nothing to put in them. She is immaculately turned out, and has met recruits many times before; always using the same speech, the same mock gaiety and peppering her speeches with French phrases*

Pickering Auxiliary Territorial Service Recruits? I presume?

Crab	Too true.	
Stokes	Yes, miss.	(*Speaking together*)
Beasley	You can say that again	
Davis	S'right.	

Jenkins says nothing

Pickering (*inspecting the girls*) In which case—Welcome to Pontefract! Now my name's Pickering. *Sergeant*—if you'd be so kind—Pickering— P.I.C.K.E.R.I.N.G. as in "Pygmalion". And it so happens that I've been assigned to do for you what his chum did for his little bit of fluff. Only quicker! Okey-dokey?

The Girls mutter

Splendid! (*She looks them up and down*) Luckily pour moi, I'm only one of a number of dedicated personnel who'll attempt—with God's help, God help us—to turn your flower of British womanhood into a first class war machine. And—drinking you in, I can only say it'll be a major miracle what will make the burning bush look like a ruddy Swan Vesta. So—pour le premier fois, I suggest that you form two's, and follow in my footsteps, as H. V. Morton once said of another and luckier leader. (*She smiles grimly*)

Private Anne Howard enters, swinging her gas mask. She is eighteen, a public school girl—pretty and appearing to be light-weight. However, her happy-go-lucky exterior hides a real hunger for life. Though she appears too dependent on others, in the final analysis she is not. Underneath, she has a strong sense of identity and humour. She wears "nice" clothes, almost too young even for her eighteen years. Her coat is a school coat. She is untidy

Jenkins frowns at her, trying to alert her to Pickering

Bless my soul—if it isn't Shirley Temple. Well, well! Though it might come as something of a revelation, we are not on the "Good Ship Lollipop" now! (*Shouting even louder*) So pick up those feet—and MARCH!

Jenkins pulls Howard into line

Follow me, girls. One two, one two, one two, one two.

They straggle out, a bunch of scrubbers

SCENE 2

Chorus We—girls of Britain joined the A.T.S., parlez-vous.
For reasons obscure and not very pure, parlez-vous.
We girls of Britain hung up our hats,
Took the oath and knew we were bats.
Inky dinky parlez-vous.

We've—wiped out the past and the slate is bare, parlez-vous.
We don't give a damn for we haven't a care, parlez-vous.
"So what?" if they've scrawled across the square,
"Abandon hope when you enter here."
Inky dinky parlez-vous.

We—took off our clothes 'cos they said we must, parlez-vous.
They banged us here, and prodded us there, parlez-vous.
We stripped off our vest and exposed our bust,
To an M.O. reeking of booze and lust.
Inky kinky, four eyes too.

During the song, Corporal Broomsgrove, a martyr to her feet, brings on a chair and a sheet: she puts the chair on the sheet downstage and takes a large comb from her pocket, which she wipes on her overall

A flat drops in with enlarged photographs of bugs on it, or a blackboard is brought on with drawings of bugs, nits and lice

Davis and Beasley enter and see the bugs. All the Girls are in their underclothes and coats

Davis Gawd almighty!

Beasley I wouldn't bank on it.
Broomsgrove (*at Davis*) Oi you. Sit.

Davis sits, and Broomsgrove examines her hair

   Stokes enters—Broomsgrove terrifies her

Pickering (*off*) Come along now—no stragglers *if* you please.

   Crab enters, followed by Pickering who is calling Jenkins and Howard

All the Girls stare at the photographs. Jenkins admires them

   Afternoon, Corporal Broomsgrove. How's the feet?
Broomsgrove There!
Pickering Just as well! (*To the Girls*) And before you ask, those delicious
   little darlings are what we winkle out from horrible heads. Contrary to
   W.R.A.F. gossip we do not allow *everything* in the A.T.S. (*Looking
   around*) Well—not *quite*
Broomsgrove (*pointing at Crab*) Next!

Davis gets up and Crab sits

Pickering So—once you are passed hygenic—or of course, deloused—you
   will then proceed to the Quartermaster's stores where the more hobservant amongst you will note a list of kit sizes. Par example: Numero Uno
   being thirty-two twenty-two thirty-four, and so on hupwards to the
   wild blue yonder—if not beyond! (*She indicates off stage to Davis and
   Crab*)

Crab having now been passed, Broomsgrove points to Stokes

Broomsgrove Let's be having *you*.
Pickering You will then step forward smartish, arms akimbo for said kits.
   And no home-darts under the bust, it being a mortal sin to muck-about
   with the *Haute Couture*, seeing as how they belong to our beloved King
   George Six. (*She comes to attention, stamping her feet*)
Crab (*muttering*) Get him!
Pickering And *you*, before you're much older. Go on, off you go.

   Crab and Davis leave

*Broomsgrove pulls the comb through Stokes's hair, then wipes it on her
overall, leaving a black stain*

Broomsgrove What's this then, treacle?
Stokes (*scared*) No, Miss. Boot polish, Miss. Dad's night watchman at the
   factory, Miss.

Embarrassed, the girls turn away. Broomsgrove finds a nit

Broomsgrove (*thrilled*) Ahhhhh! Fancy! I wouldn't have thought they'd
   have survived. Over there you—I do Gentian last.

Beasley—hair flowing—is called to the chair

*The Lights fade to a Black-out. The song "So This is the Meaning of Heaven"
is played on a record. Pickering's voice is heard as the song ends*

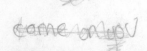

Pickering (*off*) And get those uniforms on before you do *anything.* Understood?
Davis (*off*) Please, Sergeant, where's the lav?
Pickering (*off*) No time for niceties!

[handwritten: Put back chair, come downstage take off sighn [sign] to walk rand [round].]

SCENE 3

The Lights come up on a Victorian barrack room (see set plan, page 68).

Beside the stove are two buckets. One is full of coal

On the bed down R *sits Private Lil. She is between twenty and twenty-five, a cockney sparrow whose nature would be to "tell all". However, experience has taught her to keep her own council. Loyal, her forgiving nature is boundless. For this reason she can neither understand nor accept a lack of forgiveness in others. She has dyed blonde hair with black roots. Her eyebrows are plucked, with black lines pencilled above the natural brow lines. She chain-smokes and bites her nails. She loves babies. She is already in uniform, polishing her buttons. A cigarette hangs from her mouth—one is anchored there throughout the play. When she puffs, she holds it in her palm. Stubs are placed behind her ear. Her hair is in curlers until the Passing-Out Parade*

Crab and Davis enter, staggering under kit. They do not see Lil, who does not look up

All the girls put on their uniforms. They throw their clothes anywhere. Only Jenkins copies Lil and puts her helmet on the shelf. The scene is chaotic

Davis Fancy us both being from The Smoke!
Crab *Edgware* if you don't mind! Semi-detached and a green pantile roof!
Davis East End—attic and shared privy.
Crab (*going to the bed by the table*) Right. I'm by the action.
Davis Back to the wall meself! (*She goes to the bed far* R *of the door*)

They arrange kit. Crab sees Lil

Crab Hey. You there—watcha!

Lil nods. They examine each other for "size"

I'm Maureen Crab. And that's Valerie.
Davis Davis, duckie. *Val* Davis.
Lil Lil.
Davis Where's the lav?
Crab (*to Lil*) Lil what?
Lil *Private* Lil.
Crab Like that, is it?
Lil It is. And get a move on.

Immediate antagonism

Beasley enters, staggering, her hair on end

Beasley Ei, she's bloody scalped me. Bloody scalped me *and* me so-called permanent.
Crab What's your name then?
Beasley (*proudly*) Basher Beasley at your service. (*She gives an American salute*)
Crab I'm Maureen Crab, that's Val Davis, and that's . . .
Lil Private Lil.
Beasley (*in an American accent over Yorkshire*) Howdy, folks. (*To Lil*) Hey, you look cosy, mind if I dump?

Lil nods. Beasley throws her kit on bed upstage of Lil, scattering extras on the two beds L *of the door*

That Sergeant! She's no blue-eyed buddy that's for sure. We're not slags.
Lil No?
Beasley Puts me in mind of chucker-outer at Roxy. Only not so fancy.
Crab Never did trust dentures. (*She flashes her teeth*)
Davis I dunno. Last thing Mum says to me before leaving. "Have 'em all pulled, pet—saves a lot of bother when yer spliced." I say, where's the . . .

Stokes creeps in, closing the door with her foot. Her hair has grey streaks

Davis stares at Stokes, who quietly takes the bed next to her. Davis looks away. The other girls are busy changing under their coats. Beasley holds up khaki bloomers

Beasley By Christ! If I've ever clapped eyes on't passion killers, these is they!

Every time anyone uses "God" or "Christ" Stokes is shocked

Davis (*holding up a bra*) What's these, then?
Beasley Bullet-proof bust binders! So what time are we on't Parade Ground?
Lil (*polishing her shoes*) Seventeen hundred.
Beasley Yer what?
Lil Five. And if you don't pull yer finger, Serg'll mash you for afters.
Crab How'd you know, clever clogs? (*She sees Stokes's hair*) Hey, how about that then!

Stokes hangs her head

Lil (*to Crab*) Nothing wrong with grey, is there?
Crab In its place!
Lil (*to Stokes*) So what's your name?

Shy, Stokes opens her mouth as there is a banging on the door. She runs to open it

Howard and Jenkins stagger in. Jenkins surveys the room, taking her time. Stokes bobs

Jenkins Forgive me if I'm interrupting anything—there doesn't appear to be a spare bed.

The room freezes in shock. Lil turns slowly

Lil Christ! That's all we bloody well need! Officer-lickering nobs!
Jenkins Thank Q.

Beasley moves her kit off the beds R *of the door, which Howard and Jenkins take*

Lil And if Lady Muck casts her minces to—er—her right, she'll hobserve two empty beds complete with biscuits—sliced up mattresses for the use of.
Howard (*eagerly*) Thanks.

The Girls turn their backs on Howard and Jenkins. They change, making snide remarks about them and the uniform. Howard and Jenkins are masked by Beasley

Crab (*to Lil*) Hey—*Private*. So how do you know—about that Sergeant?
Lil I know.
Crab Don't see how.
Beasley (*putting her hat on top of her bird's nest*) Ei, I don't look patch on't lass in't poster.
Lil (*working*) Poxy propaganda, that's for why.
Beasley Nay, they's nowt enemy.
Lil Let me inform you, sweetheart: from where we are—down *here*—*any* geezer what ain't us Corps, Sergs, Hofficers and . . .

Lil turns to Howard and Jenkins, who are now stripped to the waist

Nobs—Gawd's struth! Wouldn't you bloody know! (*To the girls*) Take a gander at that, then!

The girls exclaim

(*Shouting*) Oi, you! Toffy Noses!

Howard turns

Yea *you*. We might be common, but we're not Lady Godiving Muck!

The Girls agree

Howard } Sorry.   } (*Speaking together*)
Jenkins } You could have fooled me.   }
Lil Oh yeah? Well you're not at the Ritz now, and in case it's escaped your notice *we're* respectable girls, we are! (*To the Girls*) Right? What undress decent under coats. Right?
Stokes   } (*whispering*) Right.   }
Crab   } Bloody cheek.   } (*Speaking together*)
Davis   } Dead on.   }
Beasley } (*to Lil*) If you say so.   }
Lil (*to Howard*) Get me?

Howard I said I'm sorry.

The Girls turn away

Davis Dad ain't never seen Mum in the altogether, and they've been hitched twenty-odd years.
Beasley I likes the "odd"!
Davis Poor old Mum, she don't even fancy Dad's plates and who'd blame her. Nails like bloody meat 'ooks.
Crab Do you mind!
Beasley Hadn't we better get our clogs on? It's nigh on five.
Crab Seventeen hundred. (*At Lil*) So we're told.
Lil Don't be *too* clever.
Davis I wish someonel'd tell me where the lav is!

> *Crab, Davis, Beasley and Lil exit, carrying their jackets and ties*

Stokes picks up the Girls' helmets and puts them tidily on the shelf. Jenkins is now dressed, managing to make the uniform almost smart. Howard stands in her bra, her skirt around her hips

Howard You'll never guess what the Quartermaster said, "You might be size one, but due to an appalling oversight by the War Office, you'll be getting what's over!" I can't move!
Jenkins Silly bitch. (*Looking after the Girls*) Still, at least we're together. (*She puts on her hat*) As I said on the train, it's us against the rest. Isn't Lil revolting?
Howard I rather liked her.
Jenkins Spare us. (*She looks in her compact*) I must say, at least the badge is prettier than St Winifred's.
Howard Do you know, she's the first cockney I've ever met—except the maids of course and they're different.

> *Stokes bobs and then scuttles out*

Jenkins At least they know their place. Right, I'm scarpering.

> *Jenkins exits*

Howard Jenkins! *Wait for me!*

The Lights fade to a Black-out

SCENE 4

A spotlight comes up on the front of the stage, and on the steps down to the stalls

The Girls walk on to the steps, directed by Corporal Segraves. She is thirty-eight, a kindly woman who was engaged to the boy next door until he was killed at Dunkirk. She joined the A.T.S. shortly afterwards. She has no close friends, but has never noticed. She knits compulsively, and buys her Christmas presents in the summer sales. Though staying within the conde-scension of rank, she tries to be kind

The Girls stand in two lines of three. Pickering enters and strides up and down. Except for Jenkins, the Girls are a mess—collars up, hats on the side or back of the head, jackets wrongly buttoned, even some ties in bows. Davis squirms, having still not found the lavatory

Pickering Well, well. Hitler will shiver in his shoes when he glimpses this little shower! So—what do you think you are—Guerilla Warfare? DON'T SPEAK. DON'T MOVE. Because from here on in, you are miserable puppets on the end of strings—until I pull 'em. And then you JUMP. Lifeless minions in the palm of me callous hand, that's what you are. And though it's hard to credit—(*Looking around*)—in fact well nigh impossible; during the next lunar month I'm going to take what's laughingly called your "Potential", and I'm going to transform it into a "Rigorous Regimental Reality"! However—pour le moment—I will contain myself with a few gentle hints. (*At Crab*) Rapunzel will wear her Amami locks well clear of her collar. Unless of course she wishes it used as an assault course. (*She crams Crab's hair into her hat*) The hat shall— AT ALL TIMES, mark me—be worn parallel to the eyebrows, the said badge at a ninety degree angle to said peak. (*She jams Crab's hat to her ears; notices Jenkins' nails*) Blood on yer hands—off.

Pickering slaps Beasley's bottom which is sticking out. The Girls' heads turn to stare at Howard, who is attempting to join them: skirt and suspender-belt on hips, bloomers festooning to mid-calf, stockings rippling under heels of shoes, shirt bulging between jacket and top of skirt. The hat is too big and rests on her nose. Pickering senses something amiss and turns with a smart heel-click. In silence she watches Howard. Howard sees Pickering's shoes and lifts her head to see under her peak

How gracious! Shirley has deigned to attend our little soirée. Impeccably turned out I note. An example to us all! (*To the Girls*) But what is this? She is not smiling! So—I will now make her smile. (*Under Howard's peak*) Congratulations! As just reward for breaking a World Record of being "ici" less than a day and creating this Thunderous Masterpiece, you will be charged at seventeen-hundred demain. And h'in case you're wondering for what—Dumb Insolence! i.e. making mock of the King's clobber.

Howard But . . .
Pickering But, *SERGEANT!* And never forget it is: BUT, Corporal— BUT, Sergeant—BUT, Mam and BUT, Sir. Is that clear?

The Girls mutter

    Wait for it! Utter!
Girls Yes.
Pickering "Yes" what?
Girls Yes, Sergeant.

Pickering Ahhh. Now once again for Auntie, and let it ring in me ears like the Last Trump.
Girls (*shouting*) YES, SERGEANT!
Pickering And before I turn nasty—which, believe it or not, I very well might—I want volunteers—you and you—(*To Crab and Beasley*)—to chair little Tip-Toes back from whence she came.

Crab and Beasley move

WAIT FOR IT. I can get very edgy when I'm crossed. So—Fall Out.

All move

Hold—it! I didn't say the rest of you lovelies, now did I? So—at the double, line up in single file. Wait for it! FALL—OUT.

Crab and Beasley carry Howard off

The others line up and march. Pickering mouthing instructions, as the voices of Flanagan and Allan are heard singing "Strolling, Just Strolling"

Moonlight comes up in the Barrack Room

On the phrase "one I love" only Pickering is left on stage. Glowering, she marches off

SCENE 5

The Girls enter the room with knives, spoons, forks and mugs. Jenkins and Howard move the table c. Jenkins fetches a copy of "The Tatler" and sits at the table. Howard joins her with a writing-case and an inkpot. The other Girls pull the black-out curtains then turn on the light and get ready for bed. They put pyjamas over vests and knickers. Davis and Lil put pyjamas over stockings as well. Howard stares in amazement

Beasley Tell you for nowt, Hitler ain't int't mountain maisonette.
Howard Berchtesgaden.
Beasley If you say so. (*To the others*) Hitler's cooking in't canteen. Mark my words it'll be rust and rigid mortis or I weren't in catering!
Stokes (*despite herself*) But such a lot!

Lil shoves her curlers into a Balaclava—the old campaigner

Crab When I think! Mum used to cook me lovely *cutlets*. (*Sentimentally*) Everything—you know—ever so dainty, with little frills round the knuckles, and an edging of peas.
Lil (*to Davis*) Is she all right?
Davis (*sarcastically*) Edgware! What part of The Smoke you from, then?
Lil Cheapside.
Davis Strike me—Aldgate.
Beasley Via Wales?
Davis You what?

Beasley Davis—it's a Welsh name is that.

Crab Not a Jew, are you?

Davis No, I'm not. (*To Lil*) As I were saying, Dad had this whelks stall outside Aldgate East.

Lil Which one?

Davis "Honest Bert Davis".

Lil Know it well, miserable old sod.

Davis Me mum's nice. I told her. "Mum, when I'm joined, I'll get twelve and a tanner a week—and seven bob's all yours!" (*Proudly*) I've got four sisses, couple of brothers and a goldfish.

Lil I likes goldfish. What's its name? (*She kneels, spitting on the balloon part of her hat*)

Davis Hore-Belisha. Hore fer short.

Beasley roars with laughter

Beasley Hey, Pet. What you down to?

Lil What's it look like?

Beasley I'd hate to say.

Lil (*in a superior voice*) I am flattening my hat.

Beasley (*to the Girls*) Hey, come and get an opener at this: old campaigner's fixing top-knot.

Lil And not so much of the "old".

The Girls gather round as Lil watches them

Right, then. First off you wets the balloon bit, see. Spit stiffens best I've always considered.

Beasley (*spitting*) Ee, that's canny.

Crab (*disgustedly*) Jesus!

Stokes crosses herself

Crab goes out with her mug, noticing Stokes doing so

Lil (*taking hairgrips*) Then you shoves in grips like so—hard. Here. But I wants 'em back—every bleeding one of 'em, O.K.? So—when they're as tight as a dancer's dangle, you puts it down, flat like with something heavy to set it.

The Girls take hairgrips. Howard goes to Lil and holds out her hand. Lil slams her tin shut. Howard returns to the table, doing her hat with her own grips. Lil puts her hat top side down on her locker and adds her shoes round the edge. The others copy. Meanwhile, Jenkins undresses before returning to the table and playing patience. She plays cards whenever possible to establish her keenness

(*To Beasley*) Hey, Basher, you're down the wrong way.

Beasley (*turning her hat*) Story of my life!

Crab enters with water in her mug

Crab (*to Lil*) Hey, *Private*, been in the army before, haven't you?

Lil Might have.

Crab So how come you're training again?

Lil It don't suit me for Them to know. All right?

Crab What, Them?

Lil Them what ain't us. Enemy. Other ranks. Commonly referred to as: "Them" or "Them Buggers".

Beasley I likes it.

Lil Thought you might. So—who are we up against?

Beasley   ⎤ Them buggers.   ⎤
Davis   ⎬ Them buggers.   ⎬ (*Speaking together*)
Stokes   ⎦ (*softly*) Them. ⎦

Howard (*late*) Them buggers.

Lil Sod off.

Beasley (*embarrassed*) So come on, "fill us in", like, as actress said to bishop.

Lil (*thinking*) Oh Gawd—well now? Ah! Never volunteer. *Never!* Understood? Just do what yer ordered—as little as poss., that is. And not a lick more. And remember, the only dirty word is "splitting" which means . . .

Crab We know what it means.

Lil Which means, yer stick by yer mates—which don't mean pals but who yer thrown with. (*At Howard*) Gawd help us. And what's said *private, is* private, *between* privates. Am I getting to you?

Crab Like Pickering!

Lil Talking of which it's eyes wide, traps shut and snouts clean. (*At Howard*) Unless you enjoy a charge.

Davis (*finishing her hat*) How about that then?

Lil (*with a disgusted look*) Right bugger's muddle. (*She redoes the hat*)

Davis Ta. Fancy us all being Londoners.

Beasley Watch yer talk—Yorkshire!

Crab And Edgware's extra.

Beasley Getaway!

Lil raises her eyes

Crab It is! (*Boasting*) *My* dad's a commercial traveller!

Beasley All right for some.

Crab (*proudly*) It's a living. Leastways "was", till that Beaverbrook poked his nose in.

Stokes Who's he?

Crab In charge of aluminium drive, pet. And seeing as how Dad travels in utensils—well! Everytime a Spitfire flies by, poor old perisher's beside himself, screaming: "There go a hundredweight of chamber pots, and Gawd knows how many egg poachers!"

Lil So why weren't he called up?

Crab Arches!—fallen. Amongst other things. (*She winks at Beasley*)

Beasley Getting his foot in too many doors?

Crab That'll be the day! As Mum says: he's got a good position—'cept in bed. Mind, she's not bothered.

Beasley Still, takes all sorts.

Crab To make you happy! That's what my mum says.

Beasley Talking of which, have you clapped eyes on them squaddies t'other side of square!

Crab Could be worse.

Beasley Could be worse! They's upstanding!

Lil Not for us they're not—Out of Bounds.

Beasley Wouldn't you bloody know.

Lil Listen, mate, on this 'ere Basic Training, it's the *basic* they're on about. So anything what's termed fun is Out of Bounds—including soldiers. *Specially* soldiers.

Beasley Oh aye? Well them Yanks don't beat about no bush. Leastways, not mine!

Davis You was never in Yankee army?

Beasley More t'other way about, bless 'em.

The Girls laugh as they make their beds

Lil (*to Beasley*) You can forget that, mate, 'cos blokes have THEIR SIDE, and us have ours. *Including* N.A.A.F.I.

Beasley So how about pub then? (*In horror*) Don't tell me that's out.

Lil We're C.B.

Beasley Come again?

Crab Confined to barracks.

Lil So it's N.A.F.F.I. or sweet F.A., and then only cider. (*Sarcastically*) We ain't got the size for beer, 'cording to guess-who.

Beasley Ain't it marvellous! Can't even slake thirsts on ale—never mind me "afters". Tell you for nowt, I'll not last till . . .?

Lil Friday. N.A.A.F.I. tomorrow. Pontefract Friday.

Beasley I'm bloody dazzled!

Beasley pulls a bottle of port from her gas-mask case

Only one thing for it, pets. (*She toasts*) Here's to Empire Port wine and fleshpots of Pontefract! (*She pats her hair. Sexy*) Mirror, mirror on the wall, who's the fairest of them all?

Segraves appears at the door

Segraves Of the two I'd prefer Max Miller

Beasley (*jumping*) Don't *do* that. (*She hides the bottle*)

Lil winds a scarf round her neck and puts on mittens

Lil Evening, Corp.

Segraves Corporal Segraves to you—Old Bill. And it's lights out soon as maybe. Come on, let's be having you.

Lil If that's your bent.

Segraves Watch it!

Squeals from the Girls as they get into bed. Davis fills the stove

And no wasting coal—go on, put it back.

Davis But it's *freezing*.

Segraves Much though it might amaze you—we *are* rationed just like Civvy Street. (*To Jenkins*) And no sitting on other girls' beds. So—fags out, lights out, blackout pulled and windows wide.

Girls Oh no! Never! We can't.

Beasley We'll die!

Segraves If that's your persuasion!

Davis Of consumption!

Segraves And I'll consume if you don't.

Crab Not to mention "chests". (*She heaves her breasts into position, regarding them fondly*)

Segraves turns out the lights

Lil Fishing, are we?

Crab We've not all got tits like tadpoles.

Segraves Just save the pleasantries, if you don't mind.

The Girls pull back the curtains and open the windows—slowly

Come on—wider!

Beasley As the Bishop said . . .

Segraves Beasley! And if there's a raid, you wait right here for me—understood?

Davis Frozen!

Lil Stiff!

Beasley (*muttering*) As the—(*Whispering*)—actress said . . .

Segraves BEASLEY!

Segraves leaves

Lil (*shouting*) Night night, sleep tight, mind the bugs don't bite.

A door slams

She I can manage. We'll have her softened up in no time. Gawd, it ain't half perishing.

Davis "Heavy frost", it said in the *Herald. And* me biscuits have split—I've a draught right up me what's-it.

Beasley We'll not make pay day, let alone Ponte—sodding sadists.

Stokes Don't.

Davis Kipping on yer tod—it's not natural.

There is a murmur of agreement

I mean, we was three to a bed. You know—nice and cosy.

Lil Don't you get no ideas. As Corp says: it's one bod per bed, *and* she'll check.

Crab Do you never stop?

Crab pins her hair up, fixing it with a thick pink net. She stares at Lil. Beasley takes a pill—behind her hand. Howard and Jenkins use cold cream. Jenkins does her hands. A moment's silence

Davis They'll all be having a sing-song in the shelter. Mum in her siren-suit, humming and stringing her beads. And little Rosy having her nightmares.
Lil Nightmares?
Davis Playground were plastered—her arm's still a bit wonky. Poor old Mum. Got a thumb like a hammer, she has. "Sweated labour", I calls it—talking of which, these covers don't half pong.
Crab Surprised you noticed.
Lil Watch it, Edgware.
Crab Do me a favour—belt up.
Davis Belt you!
Crab (*surprised at her anger*) Look, I wants my beauty sleep, even if you don't.
Davis You needs it! (*She covers her head with her blanket*)

The room is quiet. A match flares as Jenkins lights Howard's cigarette and her own

Jenkins I must say, it's very like school.
Howard Only *better*.

There is quiet. Stokes cries as she says her prayers, kneeling by her bed

The Chorus is heard singing softly "Kiss Me Goodnight, Sergeant Major"

SCENE 6

The sky lightens. Beasley snores. Suddenly the door bangs open. Segraves enters and switches on the lights. Groans from the Girls. Jenkins, however, leaps out and does a few bust-developing exercises—as she does every morning

Segraves Wakee, wakee. Rise and shine! It's past six on a lovely blustering, freezing morning. And I want you dressed and ready for off five minutes back, or else . . . (*Pulling down Lil's clothes*) Out Snow White.
Lil (*pulling them back*) Oh Corp—how can I resist you?
Segraves Try a little. (*To Jenkins*) Get on, you.
Jenkins Jenkins! My name is Jenkins.
Segraves For the moment!

Howard giggles at her uniform

(Oi! And heave that mess under your greatcoat—army tailor'll deal with you, Howard.
Jenkins Who else!
Segraves And you!
Jenkins I don't doubt! Might I go and wash?
Howard Please?
Segraves I was wondering if you'd ever ask.

Howard and Jenkins exit wearing knickers, vests and stockings under greatcoats

More promises than licks for the rest, I note.

Lil Can't wash on an empty stomach.

Beasley It's not lucky.

Segraves (*to Crab*) And watch that hair.

Crab Everyone does!

Lil (*sarcastically*) It's her crowning glory!

Segraves (*to Crab*) It'll be more crowning than glory if Sergeant catches you.

Segraves leaves

A hooter or whistle sounds

Beasley Ei, reminds me of Barnsley, does that.

Lil (*shivering*) Lucky devils, snug underground.

Beasley All them lusty Bevan Boys stripped to cockles, right under me frustrated feet.

Lil Give me nosh any day. Come on, you lot.

The Girls run out, carrying any clothes they have not had time to put on

The Lights fade to a Black-out

SCENE 7

The front of the stage is spotlighted

In the middle of the song the C.O. enters in a greatcoat, gloves and hat. She is protected from the real life of the camp, and living in a dream world, except when she clashes with authority. As the song proceeds she mouths the beginning of her speech. Pickering stands behind her, glaring into the Stalls

Chorus (*singing*) Roll out the nosh.
                        Roll out the bangers when done.
                        Pour out the slosh.
                        Who's got the maggoty bun?
                        Zim boom the porridge
                        Cold as a parson's bum.
                        When you've had your fill of breakfast—
                        Then it's run, run, run.

C.O. —and I'm sure that by the end of your basic training we'll have turned out as smart a company of girls as this camp has ever seen. I know you'll work hard, and though the regulations'll be new and sometimes difficult to understand, everything has a reason. And with Sergeant Pickering's expertise—(*She gives a gracious nod*)

Pickering straightens proudly

—and your application, I think I can safely say that your time here will also be happy. Right. Carry on, Sergeant.

The C.O. diffidently touches her hat. Pickering salutes smartly

The C.O. walks off

Pickering watches the C.O. go. When she is out of earshot, Pickering shouts off, in the opposite direction

Pickering Right, me anguished amateurs. You've just hobserved a salute, so let me start as I mean to go on—and on—and on. Forward, ten paces—march!

The Girls enter—Crab first, followed by Jenkins and Howard, then the others. They are a sorry lot, though their hair is neat and their hats are flat. Howard is bundled together

Pickering Halt. And—face front. And—(*She demonstrates*)—stand—at ease. I said stand! Not disintegrate. Now you're to watch my every move as if your miserable lives depended on it—which they very well might! A recruit will—at all times, mark me—salute an hofficer. AT ALL TIMES, do you hear? Doesn't matter if you're starkers or on the bog . . .

Crab giggles

Go on like that and you'll be laughing the other side of nowhere. So— when you sees an hofficer—female or male—you salute. IS THAT CLEAR?

Girls Yes, Sergeant.

Pickering cups her hand to her ear

YES, SERGEANT.

Pickering Keep that up and we'll be bosom friends.

Jenkins Not if I see you first.

Lil looks at Jenkins with admiration

Pickering A salute is in three parts. (*At Jenkins*) Like you'll be Madam Lazonga. Each part to the count of three. One, two, three—up. (*Arm up*) One, two, three—hold. (*Salute*) Note the palm facing front, fingers stiff as stanchions. One, two, three—down. (*Hand to side*) The more hobservant amongst you will have regard to the fact that the way my h'arm goes up is like a ruddy rainbow. Down, it is as stuck to my body as if drawn there by a magnet. (*Banging her thumb against her skirt*) Thumbs down seams! Right! I will now demonstrate once again. And only the once. The longest way up, two, three. Hold two, three. The shortest way down two, three. So—you will now follow my every miniscule move, shouting the numbers as if to Moscow. But—let us first mark ourselves, stretching arms out to both sides so you don't knock yourselves out—before I do. AND I MIGHT. Right then—tenshun! And—mark.

The Girls do so. Crab's arm is graciously raised

Crab! You are not the Ziegfield Follies about to high kick to kingdom come, are you? Are you?

Crab No, Sergeant.

Crab lowers her hand, which she arranges at the side of her skirt, one leg in front of the other

Pickering Uncoil yourself, girl!

Reluctantly, Crab does so. Pickering walks behind the line of Girls, past Crab, Jenkins and Howard—after which there is a large gap. Fuming, she steps through it

Forming a company of our own, are we? Close up! And—arms down. And—prepare to salute, shouting the numbers one, two, three as you do so.

Pickering } One, two, three—up. One, two, three— } *(Speaking together)*
Girls } hold. One, two, three—down. }

The Girls are terrible. Silence

Pickering Yes—well—perhaps we'll have better luck calling out our army numbers—starting with Crab.

Crab W/three-two-seven-seven-four-eight.

Jenkins W/three-two-seven-five-oh-two.

Howard W/three-two-seven-five-oh-one.

Davis W/three-two-five-two-eight-seven.

Stokes (*whispering*) W/three-three-five-two-eight-oh.

Beasley W/three-two-five—er—W/three-two-five—nine—oh . . .

Lil (*fast and brisk*) W/eight-seven-nine-four-one.

Pickering What an optimist I was! For your information, we are not spotting puff-puff engine numbers now, jolly though that might be. Oh dear me no. We are attempting to identify ourself in a clear crisp manner. Do I make myself clear so that you will make yourself clear?

Girls Yes, Sergeant.

Pickering So—numbers repeat!

They do so, a little better

And—salute.

Girls Up, two, three. Hold, two, three. Down, two, three.

They are still terrible

Pickering I can only describe that as poetry in motion; and I am not training the corps de ballet de Pontefract! Nor are you FAIRIES AT THE BOTTOM OF THE GARDEN EITHER! ARE YOU?

Girls No, Sergeant.

Pickering Glad you see it my way. So—ruddy salute.

Pickering says one, two, three very quickly, the Girls try to follow

Pickering ⎱ Up, one, two, three. Hold, one, two, ⎱ *(Speaking together)*
Girls ⎰ three. Down, one, two, three. ⎰
Pickering *(looking at her watch)* Heigh ho, how time flies when] one's having fun. Company—by the left right turn. Company—chests out, sit-a-pons in. Forward—march. Left, right, left, right, left right.

Pickering watches the girls go, noting Jenkins is on the wrong foot

Jenkins! *Left*, right. *Left*, right. *LEFT*, right.

The Lights fade to a Black-out. In the darkness the black-out curtains are drawn in the Barrack Room

SCENE 8

The Barrack Room is blacked out

Distant drunken singing of "Underneath the Arches" is heard. The door is flung open by Beasley, who switches on the lights. The Girls follow—they are tight. Davis is carrying Lil. They are wearing battledress tops that bulge out like enormous breasts. Lil brawls above the singing as Jenkins and Howard go to the table, Jenkins leading a tight Howard by her tie. Howard pulls a bottle from her bloomers. The rest take bottles from their battledresses. Except for Howard and Jenkins, they undress fast around the stove: it is cold

Lil *(sticking out a bottled chest)* Tits to the wind!
Beasley Bust in the gust!
Howard *(to Jenkins)* Honestly, after matron's cocoa, cider's simply wizard!
Jenkins Cocoa!
Howard Oh, dear.
Jenkins When *did* you leave school?
Howard *(ashamed)* Last term.
Jenkins Now she tells me! Day or boarding?
Howard Boarding.
Jenkins Me too. Tucked away, as you might say. *(She takes a swig)* Gone but *not* remembered. *(At the bottle)* Damn fool Army. Trust them not to know scrumpy's twice as lethal. Specially Yorkshire! Boozy'd give his eye teeth to get his hands on some.

Lil stands on look-out at the window. Beasley hums, "This is the Army, Mr Jones"

Howard *(shocked)* Gosh! Does your father drink?
Jenkins More navigates by it, really.
Howard Gosh!
Jenkins Hazard of his calling as you might say—owns a drinking club.
Howard *(more shocked)* Drinking club!
Jenkins No need to look so stunned. It's jolly posh. And lucrative, thank

the Lord. Has to be poor old Boozer's Gloomy; what with a demanding mistress or two, not to mention a more-so liver.

Howard Mistresses! How simply *awful* for you.

Jenkins On the contrary—lot of lovely bribes, darling.

Howard is dazed

To keep me out from under.

Howard But that's . . .

Jenkins Blackmail? So what?

Crab, who is listening, smiles at Jenkins. Jenkins notices. Beasley breaks into the words of the song

Davis (*to Beasley*) Bloody pipe down. Beasley!

Beasley sings louder

Lil Oi! Beasley! Stuff it.

Beasley I should be so lucky! (*She sings*) I'll be seizing you in all the old familiar places, that this arm of mine embraces, all night through!

Stokes is shocked and covers her ears

Crab Ain't you heard what the Private said? (*She falls on Beasley*) Belt up.

Beasley 'Ere, get off.

Segraves enters, harassed

The Girls freeze, covering the bottles and smiling innocently

Segraves Right, you lot. And I know you're up to something, so watch it! Room smells like a beer garden.

Lil (*smugly*) It has not tainted our luscious lips.

Segraves Crab—off Beasley's bed.

Beasley (*in a dignified tone*) Thank you, Corp. (*She starts singing to Segraves*) "You're wonderful . . ." (*She sees Segraves' look, and stops*)

Segraves And *no* hullabalooing, or else . . . (*She looks at her watch*)

Segraves turns out the lights and goes

Lil (*turning the lights on again*) She's off to a pansy concert.

Crab opens her mouth

Don't ask. I know!

Beasley It's got a right queer tang, has that scrumpy.

Lil Ain't you heard? Bromide.

Beasley What's that when it's at home?

Lil What Army puts in drinks, sweetheart. To stop The Itch.

Beasley Aye, pull t'other one.

Lil I'm telling you—bloody liberty!

Beasley Nay, if that's fact, that's bonus.

Lil Come again?

Beasley That's just it—I daren't.

Lil Daren't *what?*
Beasley Belt em out—Me *orgasms!* Are you daft or summat?
Davis What are—organisms?

Howard is fascinated. She hovers on the outside of the group. Beasley smiles at her

Beasley Ei, hark on't innocent! For your information it's "Coming". You know, "Spending", "Hitting Jill Pot". (*Proudly*) It's scientific word, is that!
Crab We know what it means.
Davis I didn't.
Beasley I'd not credit it. Yer born with ration, see. You know, like they ration food. And it don't matter how hard you pant, that's yer bloody bag. And seeing as how I've blown more'n Churchill's had cigars, well—stands to reason, Army'll help me save up like. *Out of temptation*, that's what I'll be—like them nuns. (*To Lil*) Talking of which, heard the one about why they's always in pairs?
Lil One nun see's t'other nun don't get none.

Beasley roars

Stokes That's blasphemy.
Beasley That's joke! (*To the Girls*) Any road, tell you fer naught—I'm down to measly forty-seven!
Lil How'd you work that out?
Beasley In me hand—marked out plain as tennis court! In fact, I reckon that even if I saves meself till thirty—and I don't see it, not with my nature—I've still only got three-an-a-bit per year till I'm on't change.
Lil I likes the "bit".

Howard stares at Beasley in astonishment. Stokes totters to the table

Stokes I feels sick. I feel . . . Ohhhh. It's coming . . .

Lil moves like lightning, putting the empty bucket under Stokes's head, which Crab rushes forward and holds

Crab There! That's it, pet. Get it all up. (*She pulls up a chair and sits*)
Stokes (*coughing*) I'm sorry.
Lil Don't mind us, love.
Crab Just you concentrate. All right?
Stokes The mess.

Crab turns her face away, because of the smell

Crab I'll clear it, don't fret.
Lil (*to Crab*) Know something? You're all right.
Crab Don't bank on it. (*To Stokes*) All up?
Stokes I'd like to go to bed.

Crab leads her to her bed

Lil (*to the room*) And don't forget: them what pukes last, empties. O.K.?
Howard So how do you know you are? You know—last?

Lil Yer just do.

Jenkins picks up the bucket

Howard Yes, but how? I mean, you'd have to wait up for hours and hours . . .
Jenkins Oh, leave it alone.

Jenkins exits

Lil (*to Jenkins*) Ta. (*At Howard*) Silly bitch. And another thing: tin hats top side up.
Davis What ever for?
Lil Guess?
Davis (*at Stokes*) Oh!
Lil Or worse!

Beasley is very drunk. The others are tight

Jenkins returns

(*To Crab, about Stokes*) So how is she?
Crab She'll live. Won't you, pet?

Stokes nods, grateful

Lil So come and join them. (*To Davis*) And put some coal on.
Crab (*to Stokes*) Come along—upsadaisy.
Stokes You're very kind.
Crab Watch your words.
Stokes Honest.

Crab leads Stoke to a chair by the table. She wants to keep her to herself

Lil (*about the coal*) Go on—give it the gun.
Davis Cor I'd give me pixie hood to be down The Road in our Chippie. Ma Puffer sloshing on the old vinegar. And us singing: "Why Are We Waiting . . ."
Lil (*joining in*) "Whhhhy are we waiting . . ." Then down to the Palais for a bit of a glide!
Davis And knee-tremblers up against the brewery!
Beasley (*focusing*) Can't fall that way.

Crab gives her a sharp look

Davis Eh?
Beasley (*standing*) Standing up! (*Sentimentally*) Cycling to Heaven, we called it. Hold you so tight you were knackered on't tie pin. Then knees up the great divide!
Lil Ride a coach and pair up yours!
Beasley And the rest!
Crab (*to Stokes*) How are you feeling, pet?
Stokes I dunno.

Crab offers a bottle of cider, left on the table by Jenkins, to Stokes

Crab Come on—hair of the dog. It helps—honest.

Stokes drinks, Crab holding the bottle

First time, boozing, eh?

Stokes Me mum's a Catholic.

Crab Don't stop some I can think of.

Stokes (*talking because she is drunk*) She's a proper Catholic. Don't never drink nor smoke nor swear. And she takes us to Mass—in clean socks! 'Cepting Dad of course. Says he's drinking for rest, he does. (*She hiccups*) Of a Saturday night he'd come home—you know ... (*She looks at Crab*)

Crab nods

Mum in with us, 'case he were too gone to notice. We'd lie there for hours sometimes—ever so still—even baby, waiting for his sound on the stair. And when he got by our door, we'd go all—little. (*She makes a gesture, crouching*) Even our mum.

Crab And?

Stokes (*at Crab, scared*) Bang! (*She puts her hand to her ear*) Bang'd go the door 'gainst the dresser, mirror swinging—so we'd sees ourselves— all arms and bits—and Dad falling in shouting "Let's be 'aving you".

Crab looks away

I looks through my fingers once, and he were so—so *big!* And then— sudden like—he'd—yank Mum out. Drag her all way 'cross the lino, and her clinging on to things and crying out to the Blessed Virgin to spare her. She never did.

Stokes closes her eyes and lies back. Gently, Crab takes off her shoes and tie, undoing the top buttons of her shirt. The Lights dim

Chorus (*singing to the tune of "She was Poor but She was Honest"*)
She was young and she was frightened.
Victim of a Daddy's gin.
First he bashed and then he broke her.
Timid daughters cannot win.

The Lights fade to a Black-out

It's the same the whole world over.
Might is right, so men's the boss.
Bigger muscles, bigger build, and
Their gain is women's loss.

The Girls start dressing in the Black-out, then open curtains

SCENE 9

Segraves enters with letters and parcels

Segraves Right, you horrible lot, let's have a touch of the tranquil morts—
dead quiet, to the uninitiated, Post!

General excitement. Lil is expectant. Beasley takes a pill

Stokes—one. Howard—two. Beasley—letter, parcel. Crab—three.
Jenkins—parcel. You've had it.

Lil No I haven't!

Segraves Nobody loves you.

Lil (*flatly*) Too bloody true.

Segraves And I hope you're all replete and resilient, because Sergeant
Pickering's raring to go for an inspection of room *and* person. And as
you've not yet learnt how to stack, it's *making* beds. (*She inspects the beds*)

Stokes sits at the table and reads her letter

Stokes (*reading*) "Dear Child, Your mother has asked me to write this
letter for her. She wishes to thank you for the ten shillings and to tell you
she lit a candle to our Blessed Lady. You'll be sorry to hear that The
Home was hit, though the good Lord saw fit to spare us. Minnie
Simpson—who I believe was a special friend of yours—is now working
at your old job as scullery maid. She sends the enclosed handkerchief,
which she embroidered in the rest period. We all pray for you daily, that
you may remain in the path of obedience in which you were raised. May
God keep you. Reverend Mother. P.S. Father O'Brian wishes to remind
you of the penance you were given." (*She strokes the handkerchief, in
tears*)

Jenkins and Howard laugh at a private joke

Segraves Jenkins! Howard! Get on with it.

Howard Sorry, Corporal.

Jenkins (*to Howard*) Haven't you heard? *Here* "sorry's" not enough.

Lil looks respectfully at Jenkins

Segraves I'll deal with you later. (*She goes to Lil's bed*) Very neat. Very
neat indeed! No bulges. No irregularities!

Crab (*reading her letter*) "Darling Maureen, Praise the Lord and pass the
ammunition, Dad's gone off on one of his trips. For what it's worth I
enclose a photo he turned up. And guess what? Yours truly has a new
blouse—don't ask, no coupons. And hands off. It's pink satin with
buttons like tiny bows; so think of me at the social Saturday. Mr
Johnson sends his regards, as always! From your ever loving Mum,
Elsie."

Segraves (*at Crab's bed*) Crab—no pyjamas lingering. And let's see if
you've polished your insteps.

Crab lifts her foot

> (*To the room in general*) And remember, if any of you are bright enough to make driver, boot studs are polished ditto. (*To Davis*) Somehow, I don't think you've used your button stick on that. (*She points to a buckle*)

Beasley (*reading her letter*) "Hallo, Pal, I'm sending you—you know what —separate! Our Bett's been rehoused at number seventeen, but she still suffers from them sweats. As Gran says: Hitler's such a little fidget! Went to Eighth Airforce dance with Chuck Kaminski. And guess what: it were one nylon afore and one after as per usual. That's all for now, so keep your legs crossed and maybe this'll find you as it leaves me. Some hope! Your ever loving Pal, Blanche."

Segraves (*going to Beasley's bed*) What's this then—Digging for Victory?

Beasley It's noble, is that!

Segraves Not the word I would have chosen. Now remember, Girls— don't let me down.

Segraves exits

Howard (*reading her letter*) "Darling, thank you for your very amusing letter. Poor Uncle Charles was rather shocked, bless him, and said to be sure to tell you that a chap sticks by her unit. Take care and wrap up in this ghastly wind. We're very proud of you. All my love, Mummy. P.S. Some fondant creams, and a pound to help out."

Jenkins stares at a card—without expression

Jenkins (*reading the card*) "Ordered by Major Smith Jenkins—Fortnum and Mason." (*She examines the contents of the parcel*) Dundee Cake, Senior Service, tortoiseshell cigarette-holder and matching case.

Lil polishes her shoes, the polish bubbling on the stove. Crab is looking at her father's photograph. Davis goes to Lil

Davis What you doing?

Lil Boning! (*Taking off Pickering*) "i.e.: rubbing in with said handle of said toothbrush, not forgetting bubbling polish what soaks in easier"!

Howard takes her shoes to the table and copies Lil

Davis (*to Lil*) Know it all, don't yer?

Lil (*flatly*) Not always. (*Talking without thinking, because she is watching Howard*) My Johnny used to say he got such a shine on his that if he got 'em under my skirt, he could see me twat.

Davis So who's Johnny?

Lil Forget it.

Lil walks to Howard at the table, bumping into Beasley, who drops her bottle of pills

> Hey, Howard—got a light?

Howard (*happily surprised*) Yes. Yes, of course.

Howard runs to her bed and fetches her matches. Jenkins turns away in disgust. Lil backs to the table and takes Howard's shoes, holding them behind her back

Lil (*taking a light*) Ta.
Howard Any time—mate.

Howard turns at Beasley's shout—she has grabbed Crab's photograph out of her hand. Lil backs to her locker and puts Howard's shoes inside

Beasley Hey Crab, I thought you said yer Dad weren't in Forces? Oh my Gawd, he's a ruddy Blackshirt!

The room is still—horrified. Crab grabs her photograph

Crab Yes well—that was in thirty-seven. And Mosley's not all wrong you know. Did a lot of good, all things considered.
Jenkins Name one?
Lil (*liking Jenkins*) Yer, go on.

Lil walks towards Crab, menacingly. Crab backs to her bed

Crab Well—take Edgware.
Lil No thanks.
Crab It was a nice place before them German yids came! No, I mean it. Swamped us, they did. Couldn't even get into Lipton's for them "zitting" and "zatting" and holding us up. It was . . .

Segraves enters

Segraves Ten-Shun! Stay by door

Pickering enters like a thunderbolt as the Girls stand to attention by their beds

Pickering Morning, Corporal Segraves.
Segraves Morning, Sergeant Pickering.
Pickering Right, my lovelies. Ready for The Off, are we?

Pickering paces the room starting with Stokes. Segraves follows with a clipboard. Crab starts to tie her tie

(*Kindly*) Careful of that collar, Stokes. (*To Davis*) *Hair* on collar, Davis. (*To Crab*) And when a Sergeant enters the room you stand to attention, whatever your disorder. Understood? (*She looks at her face*) And you can wipe that muck off. (*To Lil*) Not bad. Not bad at all. (*She moves to Beasley's bed*) What's this, then? The church stall attacked by mice? Re-do it! Well, well, I can see none of you lot worked in window display—

Lil coughs

—With the exception of Private Lil. When Corporal Segraves says an inspection, she means—(*to Segraves*)—if I'm not mistaken—a well-made bed, unimaginative and sticking to the book. Not something wooshed through a wind tunnel. (*At Howard's bed*) Very neat. Very neat indeed. A pity about the shoes!

Howard (*looking at her feet*) Shoes? But—but they *were* there, Sergeant. (*She points to the table*)

Pickering But they're not now, are they?

Howard No, Sergeant.

Pickering (*moving to Jenkins' bed*) Walked off on their own, have they? Well, if they don't strut right back again, you can report to the Charge Room for loss of Army Issue. Am I getting to you?

Howard Yes, Sergeant.

Pickering (*to Jenkins*) It'll pass. (*To the Girls*) Could be worse, I suppose. (*She catches sight of a bottle of cider by Crab's bed, and fumes*) In all my years in His Majesty's Service, hundreds—nay, thousands of girls have passed through my hands, and I have never seen such *horrible havoc* as I have in this room. Never! (*She picks up the bottle and gives it to Segraves*)

Pickering exits, speaking as she goes

(*Off*) I just hope Company F will cheer me up. (*Bellowing*) Morning, Corporal Smithers.

Segraves (*furiously*) As—you—were!

Segraves gives the bottle to Stokes and exits

Lil Don't say I didn't warn you.

Lil lights a cigarette as Howard stalks downstage

Howard So who's an officer-licking slut now?

Stunned silence

Lil Yer what?

Howard You heard me. *You pinched my shoes.*

Lil Why should I pinch 'em?

Howard I don't know. But I bloody well know where they are. (*Before Lil can stop her, she dives into Lil's locker and pulls out her shoes, which she throws at Lil*)

Lil It were only a joke!

Howard You bastard! You rotten filthy little bastard!

The Girls go rigid. Lil swings round, her face haggard with venom

Lil Nobody, but nobody calls me *that*, mate.

Lil hits Howard across the face and follows through with a stomach punch. Howard buckles. They roll towards the stove, fighting viciously. The Girls are stunned, except for Jenkins who shouts: "Go it, Howard." At the stove, Lil mounts Howard's back and hits it with a lump of coal. Howard goes berserk. She kicks Lil off, leaps up and by mistake hits Beasley—who is trying to separate them—before grabbing Lil's arm and pushing it up her back. Lil screams. Everyone except Jenkins protests. The fight is very nasty. Beasley collapses on her bed

Howard You thieving little bitch. Well you can damn well apologize. (*She pushes Lil's arm*) Now!

Lil Up yours. Christ, you'll break it.

Howard That's right. So—are you sorry?
Lil Sod off.
Howard (*pushing further*) Come along.
Lil Ahhhhhh! O.K. O.K.
Howard And apologize.
Lil (*through her teeth*) Sorry I'm sure.
Howard That's more like it.

They stagger to their feet holding on to each other. They are panting and exhausted. Stokes creeps back to her bed, frightened

Lil (*sarcastically*) Going to nark, are we?
Howard What?
Lil Tell Pickering?
Howard You must be joking.
Lil Yes, well . . . (*She grins*) You look terrible.
Howard (*grins*) I see, you've managed to keep in your curlers.
Lil Take more than you to shift that bloody lot! Give it to you, Howard; for a four-foot nothing you can't half pack a wallop.
Howard For an old campaigner, you're not so dusty either.
Lil Not, am I? (*She nurses her arm*) And don't you ever call me that name again, do you hear me?
Howard What name?
Lil You know.
Howard You mean "bastard"?

The Girls mutter. Howard realizes the implication. Where they come from, it is the final and all-too-often accurate description

Oh! Yes. Of course. Gosh I'm sorry. No, *honestly*, I—really I am.
Lil Yea, well—you forgets the shoes and we'll say no more. O.K.?
Howard O.K.! Shake on it?

A pause. Lil wipes her hands on her skirt. Howard copies. With great dignity, they hold out their hands

Jenkins goes out, slamming the door

Howard's hand drops as she watches Jenkins. Then she turns back to Lil. She has made up her mind. She holds out her hand, and they shake

Lil (*ruffling Howard's hair*) Thirsty work, punch-ups.
Howard You're telling me.
Lil Right then, drinks on me in the N.A.A.F.I. So come on, let's get cracking.

They turn to leave and see Beasley lying—eyes closed, hands on her stomach

'Ere, are you all right?
Beasley Bloody delirious!
Howard You don't look all right—does she, Lil?
Crab (*moving forward*) Know what, I think she's got a bun in the oven! (*To Beasley*) You have, haven't you?

Beasley What if I have?
Crab Told you!
Howard Oh my God—I hit her! Lil, I hit her! (*To Beasley*) Look, don't
move. Don't do anything, I'll fetch the M.O.
Beasley You'll do no such thing!
Lil (*understanding*) Howard—leave it.
Howard But she'll . . .
Lil *Leave it*, I say.
Howard But she might have a miscarriage!
Beasley I should be so lucky!
Crab I knew you were. All those pills.
Lil Me sis tried 'em, and now she's got little Sid, bless him.
Howard But if they don't work?
Beasley (*getting up*) Oh Gawd—*in case*, stupid. T'otherwise it's your
friendly back street abortionist, *if* I saves the ready.
Howard But that's *dangerous*.
Beasley And if you don't belt up, I'll be.
Stokes But you mustn't. You really mustn't.

Beasley works herself up into a fury

Beasley Don't *you* bloody start.
Stokes It's a mortal sin.
Beasley (*standing*) No more than murder . . .

Crab goes to Stokes and leads her back to her bed

Crab Come on, love. It's none of our business.
Beasley Too bloody right.
Lil Beasley? What about the M.O.?
Beasley He's not pregnant, is he?
Lil We get a check-up before leave.
Beasley (*horrified*) Oh God. Can't win, can I? (*To Lil*) I'm five months
gone.

The Girls are horrified

Lil Why'd you join then?
Beasley Street were noticing. What'll I do? (*Trying to smile*) As actress
said to . . . (*She cannot continue*)
Lil Hold on—I've got a glimmer!
Beasley Leave it alone.
Lil No, listen. There were a girl in our lot—you know, before . . . And she
were carrying.
Beasley Bully for her.
Lil No, listen. 'Cos it might work, it just bloody might. I mean, the M.O.,
he's pretty doddery, in't he? And he's four-eyes, right?
Beasley (*angrily*) The suspense is killing me!
Lil Hold yer hat! Anyway this girl—the one in pod . . .
Beasley *I know which one!*
Lil Yea well—she told the M.O. she had the curse!

Beasley Don't talk daft!

Lil Straight up! It's like this 'ere Psychologic Warefare, see. You puts it in the head. I mean, there she stood bold as a brass Buddha. (*Indicating a round stomach*) S.T. like the Cenotaph, complaining she got sort-of blown up with wind when it were on her. And guess what? She got a chitty for Syrup of Figs!

Howard (*eager to make amends*) If you starved till leave, you could look a *bit* thinner.

Lil And go on taking them pills.

Howard Just in case!

Beasley (*excitedly*) By heck it might work! I mean you never knows yer luck, do yer?

Howard Gin!

Lil Hey—mother's ruin!

Howard It'd have to be an *awful* lot.

Beasley Yer breaking my heart! Yippee! N.A.A.F.I. here we come!

Jubilantly, the Girls leave

Stokes remains, sitting facing the wall

Crab returns

Crab Coming, pet?

Stokes shakes her head

Nothing you can do.

Stokes I can pray.

Crab You're a funny one.

Stokes Poor little baby.

Crab What about Beasley, then. Who'll look after her?

Stokes Our Lord.

Crab Try telling her that ... so come on, we're missing out on good drinking time.

Stokes I mustn't.

Crab (*angrily*) For Christ's sake.

Stokes Yes. For His sake.

Crab (*irritated*) Can't win, can I? Look ... (*She searches around*) I mean, let's face it, even Jesus had a tipple now and again.

Stokes nods

And you do have it at Confession.

Stokes (*smiling*) Communion.

Crab There you go then. So come on—be a mate.

Stokes (*amazed*) Me?

Crab Who else?

Stokes *Your* mate?

Crab Why not—I likes you.

Crab holds out her hand. Stokes takes it

The Lights fade to a Black-out

Stella [handwritten]

SCENE 10

Chorus We are the N.A.A.F.I. girls, warriors all. *Arrange chairs* [handwritten]
    The R.A.S.C./E.F.I. *Dress table / mime / taking orders* [handwritten]
    Heavily laden with ill-gotten gains,
    We came here to do not to die.
    Once we were honest, but those days are gone.
    The N.A.A.F.I. has been our downfall.
    We'll get no promotion this side of the ocean.
    Let's make what we can—rob 'em all.

    Rob 'em all, rob 'em all,
    The long and the short and the tall.
    Rob every sergeant and W.O.1.
    Rob every corporal, show favour to none.
    Oh, we'll rob every private in call,
    We'll even rob General de Gaulle,
    Our graft's systematic and quite democratic.
    Show favour to none, rob 'em all.

The other Girls join Crab and Stokes. They all move the table and chairs downstage, adding another small table. The N.A.A.F.I. Waitress, a slut from Yorkshire, pushes on a trolley with a large teapot, glasses, mugs, bottles of cider and a gramophone, downstage. (If a curtain is dropped in front of the Barrack Room, it has a picture of the King and Queen, posters, and a "Chad drawing"—"Wot, no men?") Beasley, already drunk, Crab and Stokes sit at the barrack table. Davis stands by the trolley talking to the Waitress. Howard and Lil sit at the small table

Davis Call this char?
Waitress It's wet and it's hot!
Davis So's Burma.
Waitress Oh aye. Well round here "tea's" code word for "water". So sup up. (*Shouting*) Last orders.

Beasley staggers to the trolley with her glass. It is refilled

Beasley (*to Davis*) Did you see that strapping bloke, by gate?
Davis Had an arse like an elephant!
Beasley (*moving back to her place*) It takes a big hammer to drive in a big nail!
Crab So—he goes to this doctor and sits very embarrassed. Then he sort of blurts it out. "Doctor, why have we got a red-headed baby, when my wife's blonde and I'm dark?" So the doctor, he says "I'll have to ask you some *very personal* questions . . ."

Beasley roars

Do you want to hear or no?

Beasley Ei, lass. Get shot.

Crab "How often do you have—(*whispering*)—intercourse?" So the man thinks for ages, then he says, "Once a year."

Beasley roars ——— gramaphone, then leave.

Wait for it! So the doctor looks sort-of taken aback, and then *knowing!* "That's it then—rust!"

Beasley falls about slapping the table. Stokes looks down. The Waitress puts "It's a Lovely Day Tomorrow" on the gramophone

Beasley Ei, that's grand. That's right grand.

Crab (*to Stokes*) Sorry, love.

Stokes I know it's silly, but the nuns—they didn't like—you know.

Crab In a convent, were you?

Stokes Sort of.

Crab I know! Let's have a dance.

Stokes I don't know how.

Crab It's all right, pet. *I'll* lead and *you* can follow.

Beasley I must tell Blanche that—bloody rust!

Stokes and Crab dance, Crab sweeping around, lifting Stokes off her feet when she does a wrong step. They pass Lil and Howard. Davis joins Beasley at the table

Lil (*to Howard*) Then that's what we'll do. And no telling the rest.

Howard Guide's Honour.

Lil Stuff that. (*She sits back and stares*) When you was a nipper, did you have a nanny?

Howard And how! Nanny Price.

Lil With one of them veils?

Howard (*smiling, then hiding it*) Not quite. But she did have a hat with a big "N" on the front.

Lil frowns

For Norland. That's the name of the people who train them.

Lil Go on! And the little princesses, did they have one? An "N"?

Howard Might have.

Lil So your nanny might have worked for your actual Queen of England!

Howard She was capable of anything. About this key impression . . .

Lil Sod the key. Does your dad have a motor?

Howard He left us.

Lil Your mum, then?

Howard That's a laugh. We're just as poor as you are.

Lil You must be joking.

Howard No, I'm not. Anyway, I bet your poor's more fun.

Lil (*flat*) Do you now?

They drink

(*Sentimentally drunk*) Funny, ain't it? There's me wanting to be like the likes of you. And there's you wanting to be like the likes of me.

Howard Which, I suppose, is why I joined up.

Lil (*bitterly*) Yea. To get away.

Howard What were you . . . ?

Lil Leave it alone.

Howard (*understanding*) Here, my round. (*She takes their glasses and passes Crab and Stokes*) Why, if it isn't Fred Astaire!

Crab Hi, Shirley. (*To Stokes*) See—it's easy.

Stokes With *you* it is. Know something? You ought to be in pictures.

Crab (*pleased*) Think so?

Stokes nods

Mind, Mum said the same. Said I had "It". "Oomph". "Personality"!

Stokes Oh, you have.

Crab Wouldn't half mind being in one of them musicals—crinoline satin dresse with a plunging neckline and masses of jewelled "interest" across the bust!

Stokes Lovely! I told my mum about you in my letter.

Crab That'll be the day.

Stokes How'd you mean?

Crab Nothing.

Howard moves to Lil, as Beasley tells Davis the rust joke

Howard Bags I get the key. I was always doing dares at school!

Lil This ain't school, mate. It's yer real life.

Howard Not to me, it's not.

Lil (*looking*) Middle-class darling.

Howard Snob!

Lil I'm bloody not. Which is more than can be said for your friend. I mean, where is she?

Howard Took herself out to dinner at the Station Hotel.

Lil Told you! Toffy nose!

Howard She's not really. Perhaps you just don't have much in common.

Lil Huh—I'm common. Got a light?

Howard No silly buggers this time?

Lil Now would I?

Crab and Stokes continue dancing. Beasley and Davis giggle at them. Beasley cups her hand to her mouth

Beasley Come in, Number Seven!

Stokes is ashamed and breaks away, running to her corner

Crab (*to Beasley*) Now you've ruined the magic!

Beasley and Davis laugh. Crab joins Stokes to comfort her. From now on, Howard picks up the Barrack Room language. She pulls stuff out of her gasmask case to find her lighter. Her cheque book falls out

Lil (*accepting a light*) Ta. What's that, then?

Howard Cheque book. (*She sees Lil does not understand*) You *know,* you
  put your money in the bank, then when you need some you fill this in,
  and you get what you want. It's jolly useful when you're paying by post.
Lil So what happens if you fills in more'n you've got?
Howard Then the bank won't pay them the money.
Lil You could 'ave scarpered by then.
Howard (*shocked*) That's dishonest!
Lil And what about making key impressions?
Howard That's *self-preservation.*
Lil Blimey, with the right words you lot can get away with anything.

*There is a sudden distance between them. The Waitress puts on "As Time
Goes By". Beasley slaps the table and falls off her chair, laughing. Howard
and Lil rush up to help her*

Waitress You've had it.
Girls No, we haven't!
Waitress Ain't you got no homes to go to?
Girls No!

*The Waitress pushes off the trolley as Howard, Lil and Davis carry
  Beasley off*

Beasley Ei, I'll tell that to Blanche—"That's it then—rust"!

*Crab and Stokes remain. The Lights change to pink, "strobing" as if they
are at the Hammersmith Palais. Crab and Stokes stand facing each other,
then dance superbly—as if in a dream. They end downstage in a spotlight.
Record: "As Time Goes By"*

Crab Little innocent, aren't you?
Stokes Suppose so.
Crab Still . . . nothing life won't take care of.
Stokes *You* take care of me.
Crab That's right, pet. (*She pulls Stokes close to her, gently pushing
  Stokes's head on to her shoulder, and kissing the top of her head*)
Stokes Maureen?
Crab What, pet?
Stokes I feel sort of—well—funny.
Crab Funny?
Stokes Sort of tingly and hot. Funny.

Crab rubs her hand up and down Stokes's back

Crab Nice, isn't it.
Stokes Lovely.
Crab There you are, then!
Stokes Know something? (*She pulls away and looks at Crab*) I loves you.
  I really do.
Crab Nothing wrong with that, Sally.

*The gramophone plays "Sally", sung by Gracie Fields, and the Lights dim to
a Black-out*

ACT II

*From the back of the Stalls the Girls march to the stage, Segraves and
Pickering in the rear. The Girls wear gas-masks and capes. They make rude
noises as they try to speak*

Chorus They'll always be an England
While there are merry quips
From leaders drinking brandy
Beneath stiff upper lips.
They'll always be an England
While sergeants think it's sane
That glory for the Other Ranks
Is only found through pain.
March left and right
Feet in a sorry plight.
Struggling on
Singing a song
Praying to die.
March double time
The agony's now sublime.
Blistered and broke
Longing to smoke
Bursting to pee.
They'll always be an England
While A.T.S. believe the lie,
That England's leaders know the best
Way us poor sods should die.

The Girls line up on the steps, Pickering on the stage facing the Stalls

Pickering And when I say double time, I am not on a nature ramble
having a cosy home chat. Oh dear me no. I happen to mean exactly
what I ruddy well say; which is MARCH one, two, one two, and no
three-four waltz holding petticoats.

Gas-mask noises

Watch it, Issy Bonn! I can interpret ruddy ruderies like Marconi and
Morse. And in case it's escaped your notice, you are not far off the
Passing-Out Parade. And the way you're *not* shaping up, it'll be passing
out into the Horrible Hereafter; because Company F, what had the
same abhorrent individuality as you shower, has now thrown it off as if it
were a simmering incendiary! In fact, Company F are *almost* good! So—

I am going to get you *unisoned* if it takes me twenty-five hours a day eight days a week, 'cos *I am not called blood-and-guts Pickering for nothing*!

Black-out

<h2 style="text-align:center">SCENE 2</h2>

The Lights come up on the Barrack Room. It is now homely: a crucifix over Stokes's bed, a vase of twigs on the table, together with a pile of books, cards, and a ludo board. A picture of the Royal Family is pinned to the wall. In addition to the other items on the table, which is now moved c, is a tin marked "B.B.". Throughout the act the Girls put change into it

Jenkins and Howard enter. They are smart: hair neat, uniforms pressed and collars starched. They fall into chairs, removing their shoes. They are exhausted

Jenkins As I've always maintained—"*Nil Carborundum Illegiti*".
Howard Eh?
Jenkins Latin, darling. "Don't let the bastards grind you down."
Howard Just don't let Lil hear you say "bastard", that's all.
Jenkins Know what she can do.
Howard It's about time you two got together. I mean, you speak to all the rest.
Jenkins Needs must.
Howard So why not Lil?
Jenkins One has to draw the line somewhere.
Howard (*in a hard tone*) Watch it—she's my mate.
Jenkins *Now.*
Howard (*edgily*) Meaning?
Jenkins Nothing. Here. (*She offers some eau-de-cologne*) Feel free. Boosy gets it under the counter.

Howard withdraws her hand, shocked

Be like that!

Lil, Crab, Stokes and Davis enter. Beasley trails in holding her back. She looks ill

They flop on their beds, Stokes going to Crab's. Somehow, she seems surer of herself, though still shy

Lil Am I knackered!
Crab You can say that again. Honest, if I'd known it'd be like this . . .
Davis Cart-horses, that's what we are. Bloody cart-horses.
Beasley Oh, my aching back.
Lil Boasting, duckie?
Beasley I should be so lucky! (*She throws a shoe she is taking off*)

Lil Want to gas us or something? And how many times must I tell you—don't take 'em off or they'll swell like barrage balloons. Come on: on yer backs, plates up.

The Girls do so—except Jenkins—swinging their legs up so that the bloomers show

Crab (*at her bloomers*) Oh—the glamour of 'em! When I think of them uniforms in that film: "Way to the Stars"!
Lil Oh Gawd, she's off.
Crab I wish I bloody were—and to the W.A.A.F.S.!
All (*shocked*) WATCH IT!
Crab (*sentimentally*) Didn't I just! Eighteen times as an usherette. When I think! All those stars in their powder blue uniforms, and yours truly in maroon gaberdine with gold epaulettes and a pillbox on me glory.

The Girls make "Hearts and Flowers" violin sounds

Crab You may laugh—but I was a dead ringer for Paulette Goddard—everyone said so. *And* I had The Tray in the interval. Right after the "Coming Shortlies", there I was in my very own spotlight with Mr Lovegrove rising up behind me—on his organ.

The Girls scream with laughter

Howard How about that, Beasley?
Beasley I haven't the strength.
All Beasley!
Stokes (*shouting*) It's not funny.
Howard It bloody is.
Lil Right, then—as we're as drained off as we'll ever be—how about a spot of poker?
Davis Where's the paper?

Howard, Beasley and Crab say "Yes" to Lil. Stokes fetches writing-paper and pencil and sits on the floor downstage

Davis looks for the paper, then exits

Jenkins plays patience on her bed. Beasley takes a pill, then carries a bottle of gin to the table, looking at the tin with "B.B." on it

Beasley What's this, then? "B.B."?
Lil Um—it's—it's . . .
Howard Beautiful Britain! We collected for it at school.
Beasley You must be nuts. The way we're being bombed, there won't be naught to make beautiful.
Howard Talking of beauty, Lil—how come your bloomers are so nice and pale?
Lil Bleach.
Howard Bleach?

The Girls groan

Lil It's having a nanny, bless 'er. In my locker.

Howard Ta. (*She collects the bleach from Lil's locker, puts it in the empty bucket by the stove and puts her bloomers in it*)

Davis enters with a paper

Davis Guess where our paper was?
All Company F!
Davis They'd requisition Heaven, given half a chance! How about this bit of duckie information. (*Reading*) "Bovril doffs the cap to the splendid women of Britain. Women's contribution to the war effort is so—(*looking at Beasley*)—vast—that no words can do justice to them. Hot Bovril cheers!"
Beasley Shows we're thought of.
Lil Pull the other one! Just making sure we'll love 'em when we're back at the sink, sweetheart.
Davis London's copped it again.

Howard joins the Girls at the table. Lil, Crab and Davis look up, worried

Lil Where?
Davis Croydon and Hampstead mostly. And Coventry.
Howard Gets rid of one cliché.
Lil Can't you speak proper? (*She puts in two Woodbines*) Raise you.
Crab You're on.
Howard As I was about to say—nobody'll be able to send anyone to Coventry any more—it won't bloody well be there.
Davis I've an auntie in Coventry.
Howard Sorry, love.
Davis No matter.
Lil (*flatly*) Yeah, well. It's either got your moniker on it or it ain't.
Howard (*shocked*) Lil! That's fatalistic!
Lil Yer what?
Howard It means . . .
Lil Oh get on with it—bloody call. Don't know what gets into you sometimes.
Beasley As the . . .
Lil Belt up.

Davis takes some lavatory paper from her locker and exits

Howard (*placing a bet*) Two.

Beasley drinks steadily, staring into space

Lil 'Ere, dreamy dreamer—Basher! Less of the gin and more of the rummy.
Beasley Shut yer cake-hole! I am attending to my medical necess—necess-needs!

The Girls play. A spotlight comes up on Stokes during the reading of her letter

Stokes "Dear Auntie Ivy, I went to the dentist and forgot to salute. The

girls ain't bad, but they swear a lot. My best friend's Maureen Crab.
She's ever so glamorous and is learning me the tango. Don't take on,
we ain't had no raids yet. And mind you go to that shelter. I knows it
plays up your tubes, but better safe than sorry. That's all for now.
Kisses and love, Sally. P.S. Maureen's got red hair like Mrs Morgan at
the 'Pop Shop'."
Crab Raise you six, and call you. Three kings!
Lil Jumping Jesus!

Stokes crosses herself

Crab (*looking at Stokes*) Do you have to? Blaspheme!
Beasley You're beginning to sound like her vicar.
Lil More like a bit of spice fer confession.
Howard (*going to her locker for cigarettes*) Give it a rest.

*Jenkins wanders over despite herself, fascinated by the card game. From a
distance she stares at the Girls' hands*

Beasley (*to Howard*) Oi—Howard. I've been meaning to ask, who's that
bloke in't photo?
Howard (*in a superior voice*) A friend.
Beasley Wouldn't have no hassle getting off with him.
Lil "Getting on", more like.
Beasley Don't tempt me, them days is over. Temporarily!

Davis returns

Howard If you're that keen, I'll rent him out. Two Woodbines a night.
Lil Hardly worth it.

The Girls protest

Howard No skin off my what's-it.
Crab Shylock!
Lil Hey, she's my mate.
Beasley More'n my cards are. (*She throws her cards in*) Who's got some
lav. paper?
Howard Lil's locker.

Beasley opens the door of Lil's locker. It is stacked with rolls of paper

Beasley Ei, cornered market, have you? (*She blows her nose*)
Lil S'right. (*Winking at Howard*) We flog 'em door to door.
Howard Under the counter!
Davis Talking of which, what's up with them latrines? They're queuing
up to past the cookhouse. For one gorgeous second I thought they were
showing Bing Crosby in the end bog!
Howard A little ploy cooked up by us atheists! And not without inspira-
tion. If most are marked "Out of Order", why then, most don't need
mucking out! Right?
Davis I could have done myself an injury! I mean *two* for two hundred.
Company F's up in arms.

Lil Serve 'em right, seeing as how they're flogging issue S.T.s.

Davis Never!

Howard Kit-bags full down the market. (*To Lil*) And "nice" girls call them Bunnies!

Davis Call 'em what you like, I'm not bursting my bladder for no heathen.

Crab Listen to who's talking! You hardly knew your way round the church service.

Davis (*walking away*) Sod off.

Lil (*to Howard*) Two bloody bogs! You've got a cheek.

Howard You'd have done the same.

Lil Dead right.

Beasley Ei, you're as like as two peas, you are.

Lil (*to Howard, pleased*) ⎱ Do us a favour! ⎱ (*Speaking
Howard (*to Lil, pleased*) ⎰ How about that, then? ⎰ together*)

Beasley Takes one to know one.

Howard "One" what?

Beasley "Survivors", mate. Like me.

Lil Dead on! And talking of which—pair of aces!

Beasley and Crab throw in

Howard Hold your knickers. Straight!

Lil Ain't it marvellous!

Lil goes to her locker for more cigarettes. She notices Stokes, who is putting too much polish on her shoes. At the table, Crab and Howard quarrel

Crab (*to Howard*) I bet you cheat.

Howard I bloody don't!

Crab Bet you bloody do.

Howard (*shouting*) I bloody don't.

Lil Shut up, you two. (*To Stokes*) Let 'em breathe, yer not dying yer locks now.

Stokes crouches down, almost in tears because she is ashamed

Crab (*to Lil*) You can be a right little bitch, sometimes.

Lil You what?

Crab (*arrogantly, beckoning to Stokes*) You heard! (*She leads Stokes to her bed. To Lil*) And next time take on someone your own size.

Davis She's so large?

Crab (*dangerously*) You know what I mean.

Davis (*coldly*) Every time.

Howard (*to Crab*) So what about our game then?

Crab Sod the game.

Lil Charming. ⎱
Howard That's not fair. ⎰ (*Speaking together*)

There is about to be a nasty scene. However, Jenkins steps forward as Crab and Stokes get into Crab's bed. No-one takes any notice of them

Jenkins (*to Lil*) I'll raise you four Senior Service to your coffin nails.

Silent astonishment from the Girls, who look at Lil, then back to Jenkins

Beasley (*embarrassed*) And Senior Service satisfy!
Jenkins (*still keeping her eyes on Lil*) Not necessarily—as I've learnt to my cost.
Lil (*after a pause, to Jenkins*) Yeah, well—park yer arse.
Jenkins Charmingly put. (*She sits*)
Lil Hey, Crab—some ain't too grand to play.

Jenkins shuffles. Lil watches her

Here, you've played before!
Jenkins What's it look like?
Lil A good game!
Jenkins (*to Howard*) And what happened to the fondant creams?
Howard Eaten them.
Beasley Ei, what I wouldn't give for Maid of Honour.
Lil (*playing*) Yer what?
Beasley (*to Howard*) Some folk is dead ignorant. It's cup cake, is that!
Jenkins How revolting.
Beasley Revolting! I'll have you know I were manageress of high-class tea shop. "Ye Olde Oake Tea Shoppe" it were. *And* we baked own butties. *And* each cake had individual coloured paper cup! Pale pink for Maids of Honour.
Lil (*bidding*) One. (*To Beasley*) Pale pink!
Beasley I were top-of-the-drawer, I were! In floral chintz pinny. Plus yoke *and* smocking *and* "Manageress" in daisy chain 'cross lapel. I were right corker, I were. Not like this bloody bag. (*About the game*) Out.
Howard You never saw my school uniform. See you. (*She puts down her cards*)
Jenkins Well, my little darlings, I have news for you. Full house!
Beasley Bloody hell. (*She throws in cards and shows an empty cigarette packet*) I'm cleaned out.

Jenkins puts her winnings behind her on Crab's bed

Howard Try Stokes—she doesn't smoke.
Beasley There's a thought. Hey, Stokes!

Stokes and Crab, under the blanket, do not move

Excuse me! Give us some fags!
Crab (*muffled*) Do you mind, they're spoken for.
Davis Want it all, don't yer?

Jenkins moves her chair, as Crab rears up

Crab In this hell I need my little comforts.
Jenkins That's as maybe, but mind my winnings. (*She gives Beasley cigarettes*) Here.
Beasley That's kindly.
Jenkins (*to Crab*) As you were—down, Rover.

Beasley (*nudging Howard*) Know what? They're loitering with intent! Get it? With—in—tent! (*She roars with laughter*)

The Girls turn back to their game. They have accepted Crab and Stokes. Beasley looks at her watch

Jenkins So how about upping the stakes?
Beasley (*leaping up*) It's nigh on fodder time—not that I can partake!

The Girls jump up and fetch their mugs, etc., then start to leave

Lil Shepherd's pie and spotted dick!
Beasley (*making a face*) Spotted dick!
Davis (*to Lil*) How d'you know.
Lil (*with a German accent*) I haf ways of making them talk!
Beasley Secret Service'd give aught for such nose.
Lil They have!

   The Girls go

Howard Hey Crab. Coming?

Tousled heads appear from Crab's bed

Crab I do not live by bread alone!
Howard More crumpet, eh?

   Howard leaves

Crab looks around the room

Crab What a dump.
Stokes I think it's Heaven.

The Lights fade to a Black-out. In the darkness, Stokes and Crab move the table downstage, then return to bed

SCENE 3

Chorus She'll be wearing Khaki issue when she comes.
　　　　She'll be wearing Khaki issue when she comes.
　　　　She'll be wearing Khaki issue,
　　　　She'll be wearing Khaki issue,
　　　　She'll be *tearing* Khaki issue, when she comes.
　　　　Singing: I will if you will so will I.
　　　　Singing: I will if you will so will I.
　　　　Singing: I will if you will, I will if you will.
　　　　I will if you will so will I.

A Spot comes up on Pickering sitting at the table downstage, writing. Her hat is off, and it can be seen that her hair is streaked with grey. A wireless is on the table

Pickering (*reading and correcting a letter she has written*) "—or, as our M.O. might say: 'As well as can be expected'. Remember that concert we went to in Sheffield, and how frozen we were? Hardly seems possible, but it was a year ago this month. Anyway, a happy birthday, darling, wherever you are, and—whoever you're with. All my love as always, Joyce. P.S. If she doesn't take care of you, I'll . . . (*Looking up*) Oh God. (*She crosses out the P.S.*)

There is a knock on the door. She pushes a photograph under the letter, puts on her hat and shouts "Enter"

    Segraves enters

Alone, they are friends   *Stroll around back of table*

Segraves (*handing orders*) Would you believe—they've upped the next intake by twenty!   *with cig*

Pickering Not again? (*Looking at an order*) Badly typed I see, as per usual. What with her and my orderly! So how's your lot shaping up?

Segraves Let's say they can't be much worse.

Pickering You said that last time.

Segraves (*as if Pickering will not believe it*) Ah—but most of this lot have joined for the money!

Pickering I don't believe it.

Segraves Fact! And if Civvies don't want them, guess who's lumbered!

Pickering That boot-polish hair, extraordinary!

Segraves (*laughing*) Broomsgrove still hasn't got over it. Mind, she seems to be settling in now.

Pickering Broomsgrove?

Segraves Stokes!

Pickering Poor child. I was looking through her file. Did you know, she was in a Home before us. Apparently her dad smashed her ear drum! (*To herself*) Funny really, I would have thought she'd have been the last to get homesick.

Segraves Don't you believe it, they're often the worst. Mind, it's my guess she'll be with us for life—if only for the security.

Pickering (*looking at her*) Quite the little psychologist, aren't you?

Segraves Not really. Same for me in a way. (*Embarrassed, she changes the subject*) Joyce, I was thinking of going in to Leeds to do some shopping. Like to come?

Pickering (*at her letter*) I don't think so, but thanks Betty. (*With a brilliant smile*) Lots to do.   *Put cig out*

Segraves (*understanding*) Course.   *Goodbye Goodbye Joyce*

    Segraves goes

Pickering sits and switches on the wireless. It is playing: "On A Saturday Night" sung by "The Ink Spots". She picks up a photograph and stares at it. We do not see the face. The Spot fades

SCENE 4

The song continues into the Barrack Room. Howard, Lil, Davis and Jenkins enter. Jenkins and Howard move the table upstage. Crab and Stokes are still under the blanket—Stokes fully dressed, Crab without her skirt. The song fades

Howard Rotten things! You might at least have done the black-out.

They draw the blanket curtains and turn on the lights

Crab Look, I'd prefer to see as little of this dump as poss.
Stokes (*kissing Crab's shoulder*) It's not that bad.
Crab It's bloody worse. Why I ever joined—tch!
Howard To get away, like me.
Jenkins (*to Crab*) Actually, compared with St Winifred's, this little billet's the Ritz. (*To Howard*) Wouldn't you say so?
Howard At least we're free.
Davis } Free!   }
Lil } Do us a favour.   } (*Speaking together*)
Howard Honestly. Mine was like some reformatory. You know, guarded every second. (*Mimicking a mistress*) "Never forget, my dear, you are a very privileged child, so no absconding to the rose garden." I couldn't wait to find out what real life was all about.
Lil (*strongly*) Misery—that's what.
Jenkins You could be right.
Lil Rose garden! Don't know yer born.
Howard (*to Jenkins*) At least there's no being a "nice" girl, amidst hundreds of other "nice" girls.
Lil (*edgily*) Oh! Slumming now, are we?
Howard You know what I mean.
Lil (*in a hard voice*) Do I? (*She turns to her locker*)

Jenkins watches Lil. Howard is upset and goes to her bed, not getting a drink. The others get their mugs

Lil (*taking gin from her locker*) Right, my lovelies, bar's open. And no tick—'sides from Beasley.
Beasley Go to Heaven on a rainbow, you will.

Beasley is served a double. Jenkins, Crab and Davis queue. Jenkins takes her drink and sits on the table, crossing her legs

Crab I'd still like to know how you got the money for booze, I really would.
Lil Trade secret, duckie. Isn't that right, Howard?
Howard (*upset*) If you say so.
Lil Be like that. (*To the room*) So—eat, drink and be merry for tomorrow's uncertain.

Crab holds out her mug. Lil fills it

Crab That's what Mum says, bless her. (*She puts out her mug again*) *And*, pet! (*She goes to the end of her bed and toasts Stokes*) Here's to the girl on the hill. (*She offers her mug*)

Stokes shakes her head

If she won't, her sister will. (*She turns to Jenkins*)

Jenkins So here's to her sister! (*She knocks back the drink*) What's she like, your mother?

Crab joins Jenkins on the table. She copies the way Jenkins crosses her legs

Crab No angel, that's for sure.

Jenkins Nor mine, from what I've heard. (*She takes a cigarette from her case*)

Crab looks pointedly at the cigarettes

Crab Smokes like a little trouper, bless her, and she likes nice bold colours.

Jenkins shuts the case. Crab is put off, then smiles ingratiatingly

Reds, blues, purples, stuff like that. You should see her boudoir! Not to mention her address book.

Jenkins Gentleman callers?

Crab Stacked like deck-chairs!

Howard I say. How awful.

Jenkins (*to Crab*) Take no notice.

Crab Good luck to her, I say. 'Sides, it suited me fine. I mean, whatever I wanted, I just let drop—casual like. And—surprise! Surprise! There it was. Sort of Lease-Lend, really.

Howard (*shouting to Jenkins*) It's still blackmail.

Jenkins (*draining her glass*) Ah me—happy days!

Crab Amen. (*To Howard*) And for your information, it's called: Mutual Help. (*She puts her arm on Jenkins's shoulder*)

Jenkins (*pompous in drink*) A very apt description, if I might say so, Crab.

Lil (*to Howard*) Like your "self preservation", remember?

Stokes It's still not right.

Crab Nor's my dad!

Stokes I wish mine weren't. (*Violently*) I wish he were dead sometimes.

Jenkins slips out, upset by Stoke's suggestion

Beasley (*drunk and tender*) Not me, love. Not me. Jack the Giant Killer, Mum named him. He were porter in Barnsley. Of a morning he'd be off to station smart as bloody paint. "Take care, Sauce Box", he'd shout, swinging down path. Ei, he were that powerful! Till he lost job, that is. It weren't his fault. Just—you know—life. But from that day on he were on dole four bloody years till Army. Tally man in rage at door, and Mum popping wedding ring out back. (*She smiles*) Ei, he had thickest, brownest neck in Barnsley—till dole. Then it sort-of withered like, veins pumping as if struggle were too much.

Howard Still. Now he's in the army . . .

Beasley I'd slipped out for fags 'cos he were going back that night. Ei, fair stupid what sticks. I were wearing my red crêpe with the rick-rack braid, and there were terrace—Bett's kids hopscotching outside number eleven—and thin puffs of smoke going up from our chimney. Straight up—like ruler. Then out of nowhere like, whole street sort-of ripped. And when dust settled, why—house weren't there no more. Just sides of floor, and parlour paper tatty in't sun. And sink leaning over like drunk —flannel still lodged under. (*Crying*) "Funny!" I thought. "Chimney's still bloody smoking."

Howard (*gently*) I expect they died instantaneously.

Beasley Oh aye. Folk never stopped telling me, "They didn't know what hit 'em." (*Angrily*) By Christ, I did.

Davis Me cousins were done last spring. Three and four-and-a-half. Took Heavy Rescue six hours to dig 'em out. Needn't have bothered.

Lil Yea. Me auntie was blown into a tree. Still clutching her shopping-bag, silly cow. (*To Howard*) And you say life's marvellous.

A row explodes from their misery

Howard It's not my fault I haven't lost anyone.

Beasley You were London, weren't you?

Howard So?

Beasley So how come you were sent off to posh school in country?

Howard Grandpa forked out, that's all.

Beasley All! With your mum tucked up cosy to boot. Do us a favour!

Howard She's only *staying* with someone.

Beasley (*angrily going to Howard's bed*) Who's got nuff rooms for aught folk. We was three to a bed, *if* we were lucky. And kid's pee stinking in't summer. You make me bloody puke. Poor is knowing you're poor, your folks is poor, and so's every other bleeder in't street. You don't know you're bloody born.

Lil Dead on.

Howard Shut up, do you hear me. Bloody shut up!

Davis (*singing*) "Who's a Mummy's darling? Who's a Mummy's . . ."

Jenkins bangs the door open, carrying a large box

The Girls freeze in case it is Pickering

Jenkins What's up with you lot?

Beasley Nowt.

Howard (*beside herself*) What you mean, "nowt"? Always getting at me, having a bloody ball at my expense. Well, I'll tell you something, it's no fun being patronized—even by you lot. And nor have you got a corner in misery or being lonely or scared or—or anything. And if you think the Nazis are only out to get you, you're stinking snobs. Do you hear me? Stinking bloody snobs.

Jenkins Quite right. Mine was done last week. (*Pause*) You know— Boozy's Gloomy!

Shocked silence

Beasley You what?

Jenkins He was topped. As in "big raid". So you see—it can happen.

Howard Oh Diana, how awful. But—why didn't you say something?

Jenkins Nothing to say, really. (*With a brilliant smile*) Except I'm madly rich. Which is why I thought I'd indulge myself. (*She starts to undo her parcel*)

Beasley So how about funeral, then?

Jenkins How about it?

Beasley You can't just leave him be!

Jenkins I expect the girl-friends'll cope—one way or t'other. Then again Mother might show up. (*She dives into the box*) Though I have my doubts.

Stokes I'm so sorry.

Crab (*ingratiatingly to Jenkins*) Me too.

The Girls mutter

Jenkins "Ta ever so". And what have we here? (*She takes a wireless out of a box*)

Crab A wireless!

The others are silent, looking at Jenkins and thinking of her father's death

Lil Yea well—I think this calls for a few extras. (*She puts her arm around Jenkins' shoulder*) Jenkins, me old mate, we're going to break the barrel for you.

Jenkins (*extraordinarily moved*) I say—don't overdo it.

Crab (*about the gin*) I'd still like to know how you got that gin?

Lil A little business on the side. (*To Howard*) Eh, Howard?

Howard nods

Davis So what business?

Lil Selling rock cakes. What else?

Beasley But they cost.

Lil Don't be daft—we nicked 'em.

Howard Steady on.

Lil And what would you call it?

Howard (*smiling despite herself*) We nick 'em.

Somehow the friction between them is made up. They smile at each other

Lil That's more like it.

Howard From the cookhouse. (*Proudly*) We took an impression of the key. In soap!

Lil And I found this friendly locksmith what was not averse to me charms.

Howard (*grinning*) She took out her curlers!

The Girls gasp

(*Proudly*) And we broke in last night!

Lil And flogged 'em—to Company—*F!*

Crab You're a pair of bloody Shylocks.

Lil (*to Crab*) And what's wrong with Shylocks?

Crab Yids! They're all the same.

Jenkins (*coldly*) Is that a fact?

Crab It is! My dad, he had a good business till they came. He wasn't always a commercial traveller you know, not by a long chalk. We had a proper shop—hardware—in the High Street. Then this Cohen opened up right opposite, and Dad was undercut till the bums were in.

Jenkins So he joined the Blackshirts?

Crab (*with a brilliant smile*) That's right!

Howard But they're torturing them in Germany, it said so in *The Times*.

Lil Howard's right! They put them in camps! I saw a newsreel about it even afore the war.

Crab Only to retrain them to use their hands.

Stunned silence

Howard I don't believe it!

Davis (*rushing at Crab*) Whose bloody side are you on?

The Girls stop Davis attacking Crab

Jenkins (*coldly*) We're none of us perfect, I suppose. (*She puts the wireless on the shelf and plugs it in*)

Crab Too bloody right. (*She joins Stokes on her own bed*)

Jenkins (*icily*) If you say so. However, I think I'll go and have a tinkle at the ivories.

Howard Like us to come?

Jenkins Heavens no. In fact, I rather fancy losing myself. (*At Crab*) Change of scene, don't you know.

Jenkins leaves

The Girls shake their heads, depressed

Davis sneaks out

Lil She's all right.

Beasley Yeah.

Lil Once you get to know her.

Howard Perhaps we *should* go.

Lil Leave her be. Had an uncle just like her—never stopped going on till he got T.B. Then it were "don't mention it"—"life's a bed of roses"—cough, cough!

Howard Still, perhaps I should . . .

Beasley She'll not thank you, love.

Howard goes to the empty bucket and pulls out her bloomers. Only the elastic and bits of locknit are left. She screams

Howard They've gone?

Lil What have?

Howard My bloomers! They've gone!
Lil Never!
Howard It was your bleach!
Lil You never put 'em in undiluted?

Howard nods. The Girls laugh

You stupid git, you'll just have to nick some from Company F, won't you?
Howard I'm tired of nicking. Oh help! Pickering'll murder me. If not worse.
Lil Poor old misery. Tell you what, give us a face pack, to take yer mind off, eh?
Howard Opportunist!
Lil And don't jam it in me curlers, they're rusty enough as it is.
Howard What do you expect, washing your hair in them!
Crab (*shouting, in drink*) I've had it. I really have.

The Girls turn and stare

Stokes Had what?
Crab This—bloody—room. Everything.
Lil Don't talk daft.
Crab No? Well that's what I'll be if I stay—daft. (*To Stokes*) Get me a bloody drink.

Stokes gets a drink. Lil sits on the table. Howard fetches a tube of face pack and does Lil's face

All this marching, marching, marching. This awful uniform, I mean smell it. And as for that blood-and-guts Pickering! I tell you, she's got it in for me. I mean, have you heard her?
Lil Yea, I did notice.
Howard (*to Lil*) Shut up, or you'll crack.
Crab I'm the one what's cracking.
Stokes (*giving Crab her drink*) I don't see nothing wrong with our room?
Crab Wrong! What's bloody right? I mean, take my bedroom in Edgware . . .
Lil No, thanks.
Howard *Shut up.*
Crab (*to Stokes*) It were a little palace, it were. You know—flowered wallpaper, and a real mahogany suite with brass loop handles. And a lamp I won at a fair. A nude. A bronze nude. A dancing bronze nude holding up a bulb like a torch. Very artistic, it was. (*To Stokes*) Give me a massage, pet. (*She pulls off her shirt*)

Stokes massages her

Over. (*Bullying*) Down a bit. Ahhh—there!
Beasley Little 'Itler.
Howard (*to Lil*) That's a thought! (*She fetches Jenkins's eyebrow pencil, and goes to Lil, but it cannot be seen what she does with it*)

Crab I mean, what the hell are we all doing here, that's what I'd like to know?

Howard Winning the war!

Lil (*sarcastically*) I wouldn't put it past them managing without us.

Howard *Shut up!*

Crab To think I once thought it'd be glamourous. You know, that film . . .

Beasley (*singing*) "A Way To The Stars . . ."

Crab Well, it *was* glamourous.

Beasley Yankie flicks is more so.

Crab (*standing* C, *facing Beasley*) Not to me, Basher. Not to me. When I think—there was something—something so "heroic" about it. Christ, I cried. But what's heroic here, answer me that? (*Silence*) See!

Stokes We'll get used to it.

Crab Used to it! I don't want to get bloody "used to it".

Howard I never got used to school. Never. I even planned to run away—but I never did.

Crab Know something? For once you're right! And I'm going! And seeing as how there's no time like the present—I'm going right now! (*She runs to the door*)

Stokes You can't, Maureen, you can't!

The Girls run in front of Crab, blocking the door. It is now seen that Lil has a Hitler moustache and lock of hair on her white face

Howard	You can't, Crab. I mean, *look at you.*	
Lil	You'll be taken in for indecent exposure.	(*Speaking*
Beasley	They should be so lucky.	*together*)
Howard	And locked in the guard room.	

Stokes (*hysterical*) Please don't. Please, Maureen. Please.

Crab (*to Stokes*) Oh shut up! (*She rushes back, grabbing her clothes, then heads for the door again*)

Girls Don't be stupid, Crab. You mustn't. Don't be mad. It'll be jankers.

Crab Listen, once my mind's made up, it's made up. So out of my bleeding way.

The Girls stand flat against the door. Stokes cries

You heard me!

Lil (*shouting*) Look, if you've really made yer mind up. I mean, really—I knows a better way.

Crab (*grabbing Lil*) You're just saying.

Lil Now would I?

Crab Too right you would.

Lil shakes her head. Crab carries her bodily to the table

Come on. Out with it. And it better be good.

Lil You won't like it.

Crab Try me.

Lil Para Eleven.

Crab You what?

Lil Paragraph Eleven—for getting out of this lot. You gets knocked up.

Crab drops Lil

It's easy.

Beasley Don't I know.

Crab Bloody hell—of course! Preggers!

Lil Right! Then when the M.O.'s sure—two months or thereabouts— you're discharged. Legal like, as simple as that.

Howard But you need a man!

Crab I know *that*. (*To Lil*) You little whey-faced lovely. (*She gives Lil a kiss*) Right then, that's it. That is *it*. I'll do it on my next leave, see if I don't. Edgware here I come!

Crab sits down. Stokes creeps behind her and starts massaging her neck

Beasley (*drunk—and forgetting Stokes*) So what's wrong with now? Lots of lovely you-know-whos cross you-know-where.

Howard (*glancing at Stokes*) It's not allowed.

Crab (*to Beasley*) Honest, the way I feel—by God I'd risk it.

Beasley There you go!

Crab And come to think of it—sooner they're in, sooner I'm out! (*Looking at the Girls*) So what am I waiting for?

Howard (*to Lil*) Better tell her.

Crab What? Tell me what?

Lil You're sure now. I mean it's ...

Crab (*threatening*) Tell me!

Lil Out of window. Round by cookhouse ...

Howard There's no guards there. That's how we did the break in.

Crab And?

Lil You're laughing! Under squaddies' windows, shouting out—quiet- like—"Para Eleven".

Crab They know?

Lil You'll be hoisted in like a Mae West.

Beasley Now she tells us!

Crab Right then—tonight's the night!

Beasley As—(*She conducts the Girls*)

Girls —the actress said to the bishop.

Unnoticed, Stokes creeps out of the room

Crab War paint. That's what I need, war paint. Anyone got a nice pong?

Lil *Evening in Paris?*

Beasley Noooo—*Californian Poppy.*

Crab For what I'm after—*Evening in Paris*'ll do very nicely, merci beaucoups. Not to mention perfume de Pontefract.

Howard Somehow that doesn't have the same "*je ne sais quoi*". I say, can I do your hair?

Crab My pleasure, darling.

Howard I'm not making a pass!

Crab You're breaking my heart!

Howard pulls an S.T. linked by a piece of elastic out of Crab's hair. It has been used to make a tight roll—A.T.S. practice

Jenkins enters, followed by Davis, who goes to her bed and reads

Crab makes up, Howard does Crab's hair, Lil and Beasley anoint her with "Evening in Paris"

Jenkins (*as she enters*) N.A.A.F.I.'s like the morgue. (*She sees Lil's face*) Good God, who captured him?
Lil Never mind all that, we've got a crisis. (*To Crab*) Which shoes?
Crab Best—in my locker.
Howard We're making Crab irresistible so she can get out under Para. Eleven.
Jenkins What's that when it's at home?
Howard (*in a superior tone*) Army talk for preggers.
Jenkins Is it now? And what's that ghastly smell?
Lil Bloody watch it, it's me *Evening in Paris.*
Jenkins Not in my book, it's not. I say, how about my lavender talc?
Crab Atta girl!
Howard (*to Jenkins, about the make-up*) A bit more, don't you think?
Jenkins (*returning with talc*) Oh, I think so. No need to be subtle. After all, it's got to show at twenty paces. *And* in the blackout.
Crab How about a dollop of rouge?
Howard Definitely. And a beauty spot. Margaret Lockwood's got a beauty spot.
Crab (*pinching Howard's bottom*) Not to mention James Mason.
Howard Oopsie!

Jenkins rubs powder on Crab's back and under her arms

Crab Watch it—I'm ticklish.
Jenkins Not when Stokes does it, you're not.

Howard and Lil frown at Jenkins

Crab (*standing*) Well? Will I do?

Howard Edgware's answer to Rita Hayworth!
Crab That's it then. (*Running to the door*) Squaddies, here I come.
Howard Hadn't you better dress?
Jenkins Waste of time, considering.
Lil (*fetching Crab's civilian clothes*) This is important.

Crab is standing c *in her bra, bloomers and no shoes. Beasley—now well into the gin—focuses and starts to sing "White Tie and Tails". Jenkins sings. The others hum, or join in, playing a comb and paper. The song is sung joyously. Everyone has had a drink and they have forgotten Stokes. Perhaps two of the Girls join arms in a mock chorus line*

Jenkins Hold it a moment. *I* know the words *including* the verse!
Lil Wait for Dame Clara Butt!

Jenkins and Howard sing the song right through with the Girls helping Crab to dress, fitting their actions to the words of the song. When Crab is ready she performs a cod "Fred Astaire" leap on to her bed. Davis goes to the window

Davis (*at the window*) Quick—Corp's coming.

Crab leaps into bed. The Girls rush to their beds and are motionless, reading, etc., almost too good to be true

Segraves enters

Segraves Well, well. We are the Goody Gumdrops tonight. (*Suspiciously*) So what have you been up to? Don't tell me.

Stokes enters and goes to bed

(*Seeing Lil's face*) Ahhhhh.

The Girls laugh

Have you gone potty, or something? Don't tell me, I'd rather not know. So whatever you're brewing up—stop it, or else.

Segraves turns out the light and leaves

Lil goes to the window

Lil Hold it—she's crossing the square. She's just—just entering F Block. Right—coast clear. And "D" Day!
Crab (*leaping up*) Over the top!

Crab goes to the window, and all the Girls except Stokes and Davis gather round. Lil washes her face with her flannel

And Up the Army!

Crab climbs out of the window

Beasley Up yours, don't you mean?
Lil Shhhh!
Jenkins Good hunting, Crab.
Howard And think of England.
Crab (*off*) Sod that for a lark.

Softly, then to a crescendo, "Pack Up Your Troubles" is sung by the Girls. The Girls get back to bed. Stokes creeps out of her bed and into Crab's, gathering Crab's pyjamas to her. The song fades. A clock strikes two

A suspender-belt with stockings attached flies through the open window, followed by a dishevelled, drunk and exhausted Crab, carrying shoes and tie. She lies on the sill then hauls herself in. She picks up the clothes and drops them at the end of her bed. She starts to undress, scratching her stomach with satisfaction. She sees Stokes. They speak in loud whispers

Hi! (*Silence*) So what's wrong with you, pet?
Stokes I'm not your "pet".
Crab Well? (*silence*) Say *something*.

Silence

Stokes Why?

Crab Why? 'Cos I'm getting out, that's for why.

Stokes They—they touched you.

Crab Course they bloody touched me. I'm not the Virgin Mary, you know.

Stokes Forgive her.

Crab Look, I don't need your forgiveness, nor anyone else's. I just need
out.

Stokes Who?

Crab Who? (*Puts the boot in*) Not "who", my little Gestapo, but how
many? Three to be exact! (*She is making it up*) With great big muscles
and great big everything else to match! Only the best's good enough for
yours truly.

Stokes That you're not.

Crab Not what?

Stokes True.

Crab (*coldly, sarcastically*) You don't own me, you know. Nobody does.

Stokes But you said—you said you *loved me*.

Crab I love my aunties, Vera Lynn, and Mum but I don't have to bloody
marry them.

Stokes (*meaning "Stop it"*) No!

Crab You! You're like all the rest. Have your fun and games, but it's not
enough, is it? *Is it?*

Stokes (*rising to her anger*) No!

Crab Right! 'Cos you wants more and more don't you? Well, *more* I
haven't got—not for no one.

Crab flops into bed

Stokes You're *wicked. Wicked.*

Crab Is that right?

Stokes It is.

Crab No wonder your dad bashed *you*. (*She pulls the clothes over her head*)

*Stokes stares at Crab, then back to the end of the bed, sinking down among
Crab's clothes. She touches the suspender-belt and clothes, then sinks her
face into them*

*The Lights fade slowly to a Black-out, as a record of Vera Lynn singing
"You'll Never Know How Much I Miss You" is heard*

In the Black-out Stokes exits, taking her crucifix with her

Slowly, dawn breaks. Hooters sound

Segraves enters

Segraves Wakee, wakee. Rise and shine. And—in case you've forgotten, we're embarking on a kit inspection that'll make Sherlock Holmes look careless, so I want shoes like shaving-mirrors, only more so.

Segraves pulls off clothes. Crab and Beasley sit up with hangovers. Stokes's bed is empty. Jenkins does exercises

So where's Stokes, then? Washing?
Jenkins Do us a favour!
Segraves (*to Crab*) And pick those up. You know what they say: "the floor's the poor man's table." So where's Stokes? Crab?
Crab How should I know?
Segraves She's your friend.
Crab Amongst others!
Howard She was here last night.
Segraves Well she's not now, is she? So she can report right back to me the second she comes from wherever she is. Is that clear? I can't think what . . .

Segraves exits

The Girls stare at Crab

Jenkins You bitch!
Crab Don't look at me.
Jenkins Something happened, didn't it? She's *never* up before me.
Howard Help! Her crucifix has gone!
Davis She's gone!

The Girls are stunned. This is the worst Army crime they can imagine

Lil Over the wall! My God.
Howard She hasn't a chance.
Jenkins Oh, I don't know.
Howard Stokes! (*To Lil*) We should have stopped her—Crab, I mean.
Crab Look, no-one stops me, but no-one. Anyway, you were happy enough to help out last night. Weren't you? Weren't you?

Silence, as the Girls dress

Fair weather friends!

Lil and Davis exit

Jenkins She's right, you know. (*To Crab*) So what happened? After you'd had your—um—fill?

Crab Nothing much.
Howard She was waiting up, wasn't she?
Crab (*boasting*) In my bed, if you want to know!
Beasley Bloody shameless, that's what you are.

Beasley, Howard and Jenkins exit

Crab (*calling after them*) Toss *a coin* both sides, can't you?

The Lights fade to a Black-out

SCENE 6

A Spotlight comes up on the C.O. downstage who is addressing the Stalls. Pickering is with her, looking like thunder

C.O. (*facing off*) I hope you realize that this is a very serious offence. Sergeant Pickering has had the camp thoroughly searched, so we can only assume that Private Stokes has gone absent without leave. Now if anyone knows—anyone—why she left? Or where she's gone? Speak up.

Silence

Very well—but if you hear anything, anything at all, you are to report to your Corporal or Sergeant Pickering immediately. Is that clear? Good. Carry on, Sergeant.

Pickering salutes

The C.O. leaves

Pickering turns slowly on a military heel. She is dangerously quiet, and very threatening. After all, her reputation is at stake

Pickering (*beckoning with finger*) So—my dumb darlings. Forward ten paces—tiptoe.

The Girls march on

And—face front. 'Cos I want you right under my nose, where I can sniff you. Hard. Now you heard what the C.O. said. Well, I'm not quite so trusting as some, and one of you ruddy knows. Crab?
Crab Sergeant?
Pickering I seem to recall that you two were bosom pals. So—why? And—where?
Crab No idea, Sergeant.
Pickering Then I'll just have to jog your memory, won't I? And I have ways, believe you me. If I have to march you to Moscow and back! Twice! Double time! All of you! Which, come to think of it might not be such a bad idea, seeing as how I was not exactly ecstatic with your turn out—devant. So—we will now commence a marathon what will make the Olympics look like a thé dansant. Is that crystal?

Girls Yes, Sergeant.
Pickering I thought it might be! So—let play commence. By the left—right turn. For—ward march. One, two, one two, one two. Come on, at the double. And give it some ruddy oomph.

The Girls march off to the Chorus singing

Chorus Run soldier, run soldier, run, run, run,
Sergeants blaspheme you for fun, fun, fun.
Forming fours, and marching with the best.
Helps to develop your chest, chest, chest.

SCENE 7

The Lights come up in the Barrack Room

The Girls flop in. Beasley, exhausted, is helped by Davis

Jenkins Darling Pickering—missed her calling, really. Spanish Inquisition? Vampire? Gestapo H.Q.?
Beasley (*bravely*) Aye. Massacre of Innocents.
Jenkins (*to her*) How are you, love?
Beasley I've been better. Then again, I expect I've been worse.
Jenkins That's the spirit.
Beasley Any road, I must've lost *some* weight.
Davis Yeah, you can't lose, pet.

Jenkins and Howard go to the table, to polish buttons. The others stack

Jenkins So how about your bloomers?
Howard Got some from that Gipsy on jankers.
Jenkins Oh? Carmen Miranda?
Howard I gave her ten bob.
Jenkins Poor bitch—it'll be the old Holding Unit.
Howard What's that?

Davis stands by Beasley's window

Jenkins Where "Them Buggers" send us, if they don't know where to put us! They're an odd crowd by all accounts. Nervous nellies, menopausal cooks, archaeologists.
Howard Could have done with one of them in our loos. I say, how do you know?
Jenkins Aunt's a Colonel.
Howard Christ! Don't let Lil hear you.
Jenkins Do me a favour! Army's like a . . .
Davis (*at the window*) Bloody hell, it's—it's Stokes. Between Red Caps! She's under arrest!

Except for Crab and Jenkins, everyone runs to the windows

Jenkins "The Swine have got Phyllis"!

Howard It's not funny

Jenkins I *do* know. (*To Crab*) I hope you're proud of yourself, Crab.

Howard Yeah. You only had another two days.

Crab For what?

Howard (*embarrassed*) You know . . .

Jenkins To be faithful, sweetie.

The Girls stare at Crab

Crab Look, the only person anyone can be faithful to is number one, 'cos I'm with me for life, so I owes it! O.K.?

Howard You didn't have to teach her.

Crab Teach her! It's the way she bloody is!

The Lights fade to a Black-out

SCENE 8

The Lights come up downstage on Stokes standing in front of Pickering

Pickering You'll sleep here in the guardroom, and be charged tomorrow. Understood?

Stokes Yes, Sergeant. But what about . . .?

Pickering Speak up, child.

Stokes The parade?

Pickering You give me your word you won't try and escape?

Stokes On the Bible.

Pickering Fair enough.

Stokes (*very pleased*) Thank you, Sergeant.

Pickering Now, I hope you understand the seriousness of this offence.

Stokes Yes, Sergeant.

Pickering Good. So—why were you on the railway bridge?

Stokes I were looking.

Pickering Just that?

Stokes What?

Pickering Nothing.

Stokes I were looking at the lines. They go home.

Pickering Ahhh! As a matter of interest, why didn't your friend, Private Crab, try and dissuade you?

Stokes She's no friend of mine.

Pickering Oh.

Stokes Not any more.

Pickering There'll be other friends. (*Gently*) You'll see.

The Lights fade to a Black-out

Scene 9

A Union Jack is dropped in front of the Barrack Room set

"Land of Hope and Glory" is played. The Girls march on, followed by Pickering. They stand to attention and salute as the C.O. enters. Then the Girls march down the steps, around the Stalls, and back on stage. They have ramrod backs and march with precision. Lil's hair is out of curlers—frizzing upwards in manic freedom. For the first time they are a perfectly drilled unit: faceless soldiers instead of a group of individuals. As the music ends they pass the C.O., saluting

Pickering Company—halt! *face ~~front~~ front*

The C.O. addresses them

C.O. This is indeed a proud day for all of us. You have now completed your basic training, and after your well-earned leave you will join your units to play your part in our Country's struggle for freedom. And never forget that each and every one of you has a real contribution to make to the Victory that will indeed be ours.

Beasley faints. No-one moves

I know that you will often be tired and bored; you will ask yourselves how regular filing can help the war effort. But never forget that a chain is as strong as its weakest link, and without the small fleet of boats, the great army at Dunkirk would have perished on the beaches of— (*disapprovingly*)—France! With this in mind, I now ask you always to bear yourselves as efficiently as you do today. I am very proud to be the Commanding Officer of such a smart and alert part of the Auxiliary Territorial Service. Thank you.

During the speech the Girls straighten proudly. Pickering looks at them and actually smiles: she is already thinking of the next intake. At the end of the speech the C.O. salutes. All return the salute

The C.O. wanders off

Pickering (*as the C.O. goes*) Eyes—right. (*After the C.O. has gone*) Eyes front. Company—by the left, right turn. Quick march.

The Girls march off, stepping over Beasley

The Lights fade to a Black-out. In the darkness the table and two chairs are moved downstage

SCENE 10

A table and two chairs are set downstage to represent Pickering's office

Pickering enters. There is a knock on a door offstage

Pickering Enter.

Stokes enters

Well, Private Stokes?

Stokes Sergeant.

Pickering At ease. In fact I think we might sit. Even Sergeants get tired sometimes.

They sit. Pickering removes her hat

I hope you realize how lenient the C.O.'s been.

Stokes Yes, Sergeant.

Pickering Good. Now—I see from your file that The Home—

Stokes looks up

—trained you for domestic service.

Stokes Yes, Sergeant.

Pickering And how do you feel about that?

Stokes About what?

Pickering Housework?

Stokes It's all I know.

Pickering Fair enough. Your posting's come through, and—um—you're to stay here. (*Embarrassed*) It just so happens that I need an orderly, and you fill the bill.

Stokes Yes, Sergeant.

Pickering Don't object, do you?

Stokes Oh no. I mean, I likes it here. Least till . . .

Pickering Quite. You see my—um—last one, had to go home—mother poorly.

Stokes Poor girl.

Pickering Indeed. So—apply yourself, Stokes, and I'm sure you'll settle in nicely.

Stokes Oh, I will. I really will.

Pickering That's the spirit! (*Silence*) Er—cigarette? Come—we're not on duty now. Not now we're relaxez-vousing. Seated!

Stokes (*taking the cigarette packet and extracting one*) Thanks.

Pickering (*heartily*) That's more like it.

Pickering lights the cigarette attentively

And if you really want to please me, I like my room neat as my person, and a good strong cuppa first thing. None of your N.A.A.F.I. muck.

Stokes I'll do my best.
Pickering (*after a pause*) I do believe you will. (*She stands, touching Stokes' shoulders*) She wasn't worth it.
Stokes No.
Pickering Good girl.

Stokes holds out the cigarettes

Stokes Your cigarettes.
Pickering Keep 'em. Here. (*She hands Stokes the matches*)
Stokes Ta. And for the job.
Pickering Job? Oh, nothing to thank me for. Right. Off you go.

Stokes stands and stubs out her cigarette

One thing, you don't happen to enjoy music, do you?
Stokes Oh yes, Sergeant. Very much.
Pickering (*smiling*) I thought you might.

Stokes exits

Pickering hums to herself, "Lily of Laguna"—"She's my lady love, she is my . . .", etc. The Lights fade to a Black-out. In the darkness the table and chairs are reset, and the "B.B." tin placed on Lil's locker

KILL me!

Scene 11

The Lights come up in the Barrack Room. It is empty except for Crab sitting on her bed and staring into space. When the Girls come in they ignore her

Jenkins and Howard enter. They are in a happy mood. They take off their ties, etc. Howard gets the drink and they fetch their mugs

Howard Pity about Company F.
Jenkins Who could have been so beastly as to put lard in their boot polish?
Howard Doesn't bear thinking about.

Lil and Davis enter

Lil Hey—guess who's been posted to a gunsite, *and* within striking distance of London!
Jenkins Not with your gun, I hope?
Lil Yeah, well—better watch it! (*To Davis*) Come to think of it, there's a load of soldiers down Guildford way.
Davis Yer just saying.
Lil I were evacuated there, duckie. Me and me sis.
Davis You never talks about your family.
Lil We were born! And now I'm bursting to pee. (*She takes lavatory paper from her locker*)

Jenkins Tonight, darling, the loos are your oyster.
Lil Cheeky bitch!

Lil exits

Howard (*calling after her*) Some other poor sod'll clean them, 'cos I'll be
   driving.
Jenkins *Et moi*. Mind, I'll be superb behind the wheel—though I have
   grave doubts about Bugatti Howard.

Howard gives Jenkins the "up yours" sign

   Beasley enters, exhausted and very down. She half smiles at Crab

Beasley You and your slimming! I could have snuffed it, fainting ont'
   concrete. No wonder it's called the Passing-Out Parade.
Davis Poor old perisher.
Howard So come on, what happened with old four-eyes?

The Girls remember and freeze

Beasley (*flatly*) I did what you said—every last instruction. March in bold
   as brass Buddha. Stood four-square. The lot. Know what he said?
Jenkins (*closing her eyes*) I can't bear it.
Beasley A1 Beasley! Though I suggest you take off some weight.

The Girls congratulate her

Howard Oh Basher—you must be thrilled. (*She pours drinks and starts to
   hand them out*)
Beasley I'm chuffed to buggery. (*She lets out her skirt*) Ei, that's more like
   it.
Crab I'm very happy for you, Basher.

The Girls glance at Crab

   Lil enters

Beasley There's kindly, Crab, and why don't you . . . (*come and join*)
Lil Shut up!
Howard (*jumping in. To Lil*) Guess what—Beasley's passed her medical!
Lil Told you! Oh Basher, that's great. Really great.
Beasley It were your idea, pet.
Howard (*toasting*) Right then: here's to Beasley, and may all her problems
   be little ones.
Beasley Do you mind!
Lil And a little less active service.
Beasley Too right. Mind, when I ponder. In t'Germany I'd have got a
   medal. One of Hitler's mothers, that's what I'd have been. But—from
   here on in, I do *my* bit and *not* theirs. (*She goes to the wireless*) All right?
   So sod the bishop—
Girls —and the actress!
Beasley And talking of "bits", guess where I've been posted. (*She turns on
   the wireless*)
Jenkins Maidenhead?

Beasley You can be very coarse! Llandudno-by-Sea—as trainee canteen manageress!
Jenkins Casting your cup cakes on the water, no doubt.
Beasley (*drunk again*) If I have the mind!
Davis Army Education. Sod that for a lark.
Crab (*viciously, from her bed*). Didn't know you could read.
Davis (*viciously*) But *London*, duckie.

The wireless warms up. Jenkins listens first. She shouts to the others to "belt up". They are startled by her tone and words, and are silent. They are very shocked, and even Beasley focuses. Crab looks at the others and then lowers her head. The following voices come from the loudspeaker

Intelligence Officer . . . the dead could be as high as millions.
Interviewer Come, surely that's an exaggeration?
Intelligence Officer On the contrary, one of our men reported that the stench of burning flesh can be smelt . . .
Interviewer Please! Some of our Jewish listeners have relatives who are being held.
Intelligence Officer Just so long as no-one believes it's not happening, that's all. Together with medical experiments—so called—and gas chambers, and . . .

Davis switches off the wireless, her back to the room

Davis That's what you get for being one of the chosen people.
Lil Yer what?
Davis Didn't yer know—I'm one of them! A bloody four-by-two. Jewess. (*at Crab*) Yid!
Crab Jesus!
Davis Him too.
Beasley But—but why . . .?
Davis Didn't I let on? Silly really, but when I joined up like—I thought it'd be nice not to feel—different. And it were.
Beasley But we're all the same in here.
Davis (*in a hard voice*) But not *out there*. Leastways not . . . Remember Mosley's gang afore the war?
Lil Don't I just.
Davis Yeah, well—one night—it were nothing special—usual Saturday. Me and me dad on the stall—you know—customers ten deep yelling for service. Then—the road sort of empties. And we heard 'em. By God, we did. I saw this bloke I knew—Fred Bramwell from the corner shop what sold me sweets and did up me sandal. They smashed every bloody thing—crates, stall, handcart—Dad.

Silence

Crab I said things—even at school. Awful things, like . . .
Davis I've heard 'em all.
Crab What must you think?
Davis Don't matter.

Crab It *does*.

Davis You're not *that* bad, compared with some 'sides, mates is who you're thrown with, right?

Crab (*amazed*) And we are? Mates?

Davis 'Course. What else? (*To the rest of the Girls. Hard*) What else, eh? (*She stares at them*)

The Girls nod, except for Lil

(*In a hard voice*) Lil?

Lil nods

(*To Crab*) See?

Crab (*going to Davis*) Oh Val! Oh Val, I loves you. I really do. (*She hugs Davis*)

Davis Bloody watch it. I'm not Stokes.

Crab (*standing*) Bugger Hitler, that's what I say!

Davis I'll drink to that, but Gawd I will.

Crab (*toasting*) Bugger Hitler.

Unlike the toast to Beasley, the answers are quiet and serious

All Bugger Hitler.

Davis So where are you off to, then?

Crab Don't ask—Orkneys!

The Girls roar with laughter, it breaks the tension. Lil picks up her towel and goes to the door

Howard I say, Lil, you're not actually going to wash? I mean, that and the curlers! Are you sure it's wise?

Lil It *is* our last night.

Lil exits

It reminds the Girls, and they are quiet as they take their bits off the wall and undress. Crab fetches her flowers and gives them to Davis. Beasley remains at the table drinking. Jenkins fetches a blanket and puts it round her shoulders before joining her

Howard Mummy's saved up three weeks' meat ration! We're having roast beef and Yorkshire pudding.

Jenkins Personally, I've had enough of Yorkshire to last a lifetime.

Beasley Hey up!

Howard Oh, I don't know. One day we might all long to be back again. You know, when we're old. Forty!

Davis Yea. Wonder where we'll be?

Jenkins Dead probably.

Beasley Never.

Howard Might. I mean, by the law of averages.

Davis (*happily*) Don't talk daft. We'll be spliced, with lots of rowdy kids.

Beasley With middle-age spread.

Jenkins You've got that already.

Lil enters

Lil Wouldn't you know! Company F's puked all over the floor. So what you on about?
Crab The future.
Lil Oh that.
Jenkins Ghastly crow's feet and grey hair.
Howard Like Stokes—the hair, I mean. She won't marry. I wonder who I'll marry?
Lil Some posh git with an Oxford accent.
Davis We'll pass in the street and not even know each other.
Lil (*at Howard*) Or want to.
Howard Don't be silly.
Lil (*seriously*) I wonder.
Beasley What is this? A bum's rush? We're meant to be celebrating, aren't we? Well if you're going to be such a load of Misery Martins, I'm flaking. (*She tries to get up and falls back*)
Jenkins Come along, me old Basher. Beddie bies.

They stagger to Beasley's bed, singing "Strolling, just strolling, by the light of the silvery moon . . ."

Beasley Know summat? I'm going to miss you lot.
Jenkins How extraordinary. So am I! (*She sees the "B.B." tin on Lil's locker*) Hey Lil, what about the collection?
Lil Oh Gawd—yes. (*She stands on her bed, holding the tin*) Beasley, me old lovely—B.B. does not stand for "Beautiful Britain". It—stands—for . . .
All Beasley's Bortion!

Lil gives Beasley the tin. She shakes it, then opens it and takes out some silver and a five pound note. She starts to cry

Beasley Ei—nay! A fiver! (*To Jenkins*) Yer silly cow.
Jenkins You too. So come along—beddie bies.

Segraves enters

Segraves So—we've got shot of you lot. And I must say, you look a right beautiful bevy. Now don't forget, travel warrants first thing. So, sleep tight and no hullabalooing, or . . .
All ELSE!
Lil We love you, Corp.
Segraves That'll be the day. In a week's time you won't even remember what I look like—but thanks all the same. You're a good bunch.
Lil Of scrubbers.
Segraves (*after a pause*) Aren't we all.

Segraves opens the curtains, turns out the light and exits

Silence

Davis It's not like I imagined—our last night.
Lil Nothing ever is, pet. So . . . night night.
All Night night.

Howard And don't forget—we're all meeting at Lyons Corner House, first of January, nineteen forty-six, at one o'clock.

Jenkins I wouldn't bank on it.

Music is heard—"Lily of Laguna"

Howard (*at Lil's bed*) Lil? Are you asleep?

Lil Yeah. (*She pats the bed*) Come 'ere. (*She lights a cigarette*)

Howard I won't tell. Promise.

Lil Tell what?

Howard You know. What happened. Before.

Lil Cross yer heart?

Howard 'Course.

Lil (*giving the cigarette to Howard*) I were spliced.

Howard Gosh!

Lil (*tenderly*) My Johnny.

Howard But—what happened?

Lil Met someone, didn't I? Didn't love him, nor nothing. But—you know how it is. Hubby off fighting, and him about to get shipped. (*She takes back the cigarette*) Anyway, we bunked up—just the once. And my Johnny—he gets leave. Unexpected like. Wouldn't have nothing to do with me after that. Not a peep. Nor the family.

Howard Why ever not?

Lil Shamed 'em, didn't I.

Howard So that's why you didn't get any letters!

Lil Yep.

Howard And why you left the army.

Lil What?

Howard Being married.

Lil Do us a favour. Got preggers, see. Mind, I lost the little chap. Big raid on the docks. Two days' old he were—hadn't even got his eyes open.

Howard Oh, Lil.

Lil Know something? There is survivors, and there is survivors. And for some of us—well—we're fucked up 'afore we start. (*She stubs out her cigarette and pulls the blankets over her head*)

The Lights fade to a Black-out

EPILOGUE

This is heard on the front-of-the-house loudspeakers

Chorus (*singing softly*)
> The A.T.S. went in to fight, parlez vous.
> The A.T.S. went in to fight, parlez vous.
> The A.T.S. went in to fight,
> (*Loudly*)

SOME WERE WRONG, BUT MOST WERE RIGHT.
Inky, dinky, *up yours too!*

A Light glows through the open door

Segraves (*off*) W/eight-two-seven-five, Segraves.
Voice (*off*) Retired Sergeant-Major. Shares a house with her sister.

The Light is stronger, streaking across the floor from the door

Pickering (*off*) W/two-oh-five-nine, Pickering.
Voice (*off*) County Council Advisor on Music. Admitted to Geriatric
   Ward, nineteen seventy-six.

As each name is called the Light becomes brighter

Howard (*off*) W/three-two-seven-five-oh-one, Howard.
Voice (*off*) Married to the man in the photograph. Lives in London.
   Writer.
Davis (*off*) W/three-two-five-two-eight-seven, Davis.
Voice (*off*) Married with four children. Charring and nursing Dad.
Jenkins (*off*) W/three-two-seven-five-oh-two, Jenkins.
Voice (*off*) Married. Divorced. Married. Pineapple farming in the Virgin
   Islands.
Lil (*off*) W/eight-seven-nine-four-one, Private Lil.
Voice (*off*) Orderly in Children's Hospital. Now housebound with
   arthritis.
Stokes (*off*) W/three-three-five-two-eight-oh, Stokes.
Voice (*off*) O.B.E. Warden of Home for Unmarried Mothers.
Crab (*off*) W/three-two-seven-seven-four-eight, Crab.
Voice (*off*) G.I. Bride. Separated. Runs a motel in Illinois.

The Light fades. Pause

Segraves (*off*) Beasley! Beasley!
Pickering (*flat voice, off*) Died, nineteen forty-four, while on leave from
   the A.T.S. Cause of death: Septicaemia following an illegal abortion.

The "Last Post" sounds, as the Light fades to a Black-out

FURNITURE AND PROPERTY LIST

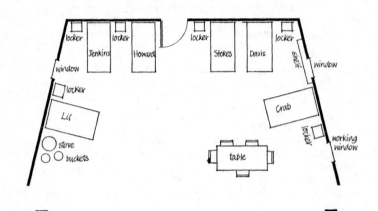

ACT I

On stage: 6 beds with bedding
6 lockers
Table
5 small chairs
Stove
2 buckets. *In one:* coal
Blackout curtains

Off stage: Chair, (sheet) **(Broomsgrove)**
Blackboard, or photographs on flat
Jug of water (for **Crab** to fill mug)
7 letters, 2 parcels **(Segraves)**
In **Stokes's** *letter:* handkerchief
In **Howard's** *letter:* fondant creams, pound note
In **Jenkins's** *parcel:* cake, Senior Service cigarettes, cigarette holder and case of tortoiseshell
In **Crab's** *letter:* photograph
Clipboard **(Pickering)**
Small table
Trolley with teapot, glasses, mugs, bottles of cider, gramophone, records

Personal (ACTS I and II)

Crab: gas-mask, umbrella, army kit, knife, spoon, fork, mug, hairgrips, pink hairnet, bottle of cider

Beasley: gas-mask, chewing-gum, army kit, knife, fork, spoon, mug, hairgrips, bottle of port (for gas-mask case), bottle of pills, bottle of cider, empty cigarette packet, watch.

Stokes: gas-mask, carrier bag with sandwiches, combinations, Bible, rosary, crucifix, army kit, silver hairspray, knife, spoon, fork, mug, hairgrips

Davis: gas-mask, army kit, knife, fork, spoon, mug, hairgrips, bottle of cider

Jenkins: gas-mask, army kit, handbag with make-up accessories, knife, spoon, fork, mug, copy of *Tatler*, hairgrips, playing-cards, cold cream, cigarettes, matches, bottle of cider, eau-de-Cologne

Howard: gas-mask, army kit, handbag with make-up accessories, knife, fork, spoon, mug, writing-case, inkpot, hairgrips, cold cream, cigarettes, matches, bottle of cider, lighter, cheque-book and oddments (for gas-mask case)

Lil: cigarettes, matches, army kit, curlers, knife, fork, spoon, mug, gas-mask, hairgrips, bottle of cider

Broomsgrove: comb

Pickering: watch, cigarettes, matches

Segraves: watch

ACT II

Strike: Bottles, letters, papers, etc.
Small table

Set: Room generally more tidy and homely
Bucket back in place. *In it:* trick pair of torn bloomers
Re-set table and chairs. *On table:* vase of twigs, pile of books, playing-cards, ludo board, "B.B." tin with coins and note inside
All mugs in respective lockers
Picture of Royal Family on wall, together with other personal pictures and decorations
Crucifix over **Stokes's** bed
In Stokes's locker: writing-paper, pencil
In Beasley's locker: bottle of gin, stacks of lavatory paper
In Lil's locker bleach, cigarettes, bottle of gin, bottle of scent, lavatory paper
In Davis's locker: lavatory paper
In Howard's locker: tube of face pack, bottle of drink, towel
In Jenkins's locker: eyebrow pencil, talc
In Crab's locker: civilian clothes, best shoes
In all lockers: clothing and general dressing

Off stage: Newspaper (**Davis**)
Wireless set, pen, paper, photograph (**Pickering**)
Order papers (**Segraves**)
Box containing wireless set (**Jenkins**)
Union Jack cloth

LIGHTING PLOT

Property fittings required: 2 pendants
Interior. A barrack room, and small insets

ACT I

To open: Lights up on downstage area

Cue 1	**Girls** exit *Dim lighting generally*	(Page 3)
Cue 2	At end of song *Return to opening lighting*	(Page 3)
Cue 3	**Beasley** sits to have hair examined *Fade to Black-out*	(Page 4)
Cue 4	**Pickering:** "No time for niceties." *Lights up on Barrack Room: day*	(Page 5)
Cue 5	**Howard:** "Jenkins! *Wait for me!*" *Fade to Black-out, then bring up lighting on downstage area*	(Page 8)
Cue 6	**Song on Record:** "With the Light of the Moon Above." *Cross-fade to moonlight in barrack room*	(Page 10)
Cue 7	**Girls** turn on lights *Snap on pendants and interior lighting*	(Page 10)
Cue 8	**Segraves** turns off lights *Snap off pendants and covering lighting*	(Page 14)
Cue 9	**Girls** open black-out curtains *Bring up moonlight in barrack room*	(Page 14)
Cue 10	At end of SCENE 5 *Bring up dawn effect, followed by pendants when* **Segraves** *turns on lights*	(Page 15)
Cue 11	**Lil:** "Come on, you lot." *Fade to Black-out, then bring up downstage lighting*	(Page 16)
Cue 12	**Pickering:** "*Left*, right. *Left*, right." *Fade to Black-out*	(Page 19)
Cue 13	**Beasley** turns on lights *Snap on pendants and covering lighting*	(Page 19)
Cue 14	**Segraves** turns out lights *Snap off pendants and covering lighting*	(Page 20)
Cue 15	**Lil** turns on lights *Repeat Cue 12*	(Page 20)
Cue 16	**Crab** undresses **Stokes** *Slow fade to Black-out*	(Page 23)

Cue 37	**Pickering** hums "Lily of Laguna" *Fade to Black-out, then bring up Barrack Room lighting:* *night, pendants on*	(Page 61)
Cue 38	**Segraves** turns out lights and opens curtains *Cross-fade to moonlight effect*	(Page 65)
Cue 39	**Lil** pulls blankets over her head *Fade to Black-out*	(Page 66)
Cue 40	**Chorus:** " . . . *up yours too!*" *Beam of light through open doorway. As each name is called* *the light grows stronger*	(Page 67)
Cue 41	**Voice** (*off*): ". . . runs a motel in Illinois." *Light dims, fading to Black-out as "Last Post" sounds*	(Page 67)

EFFECTS PLOT

ACT I

Cue 1 As **Girls** line up in Scene 4   (Page 9)
Hooter sounds

Cue 2 After **Segraves** exits   (Page 14)
Door slams

Cue 3 After **Segraves** leaves   (Page 16)
Hooter sounds

ACT II

Cue 1 After "Pack Up Your Troubles" song fades   (Page 53)
Clock strikes two

Cue 2 As Lights come up to dawn   (Page 55)
Hooter sounds

Cue 3 **Davis:** "But *London*, duckie."   (Page 63)
Voices from wireless loudspeaker